T0222490

Maker Innovations Series

Jump start your path to discovery with the Apress Maker Innovations series! From the basics of electricity and components through to the most advanced options in robotics and Machine Learning, you'll forge a path to building ingenious hardware and controlling it with cutting-edge software. All while gaining new skills and experience with common toolsets you can take to new projects or even into a whole new career.

The Apress Maker Innovations series offers projects-based learning, while keeping theory and best processes front and center. So you get hands-on experience while also learning the terms of the trade and how entrepreneurs, inventors, and engineers think through creating and executing hardware projects. You can learn to design circuits, program AI, create IoT systems for your home or even city, and so much more!

Whether you're a beginning hobbyist or a seasoned entrepreneur working out of your basement or garage, you'll scale up your skillset to become a hardware design and engineering pro. And often using low-cost and open-source software such as the Raspberry Pi, Arduino, PIC microcontroller, and Robot Operating System (ROS). Programmers and software engineers have great opportunities to learn, too, as many projects and control environments are based in popular languages and operating systems, such as Python and Linux.

If you want to build a robot, set up a smart home, tackle assembling a weather-ready meteorology system, or create a brand-new circuit using breadboards and circuit design software, this series has all that and more! Written by creative and seasoned Makers, every book in the series tackles both tested and leading-edge approaches and technologies for bringing your visions and projects to life.

More information about this series at https://link.springer.com/bookseries/17311

ABCs of Electronics

An Easy Guide to Electronics Engineering

Farzin Asadi

Apress®

ABCs of Electronics: An Easy Guide to Electronics Engineering

Farzin Asadi
Department of Electrical and Electronics Engineering,
Maltepe University,
Istanbul, Türkiye

Department of Electrical and Electronics Engineering,
Beykent University,
Istanbul, Türkiye

ISBN-13 (pbk): 979-8-8688-0133-4   ISBN-13 (electronic): 979-8-8688-0134-1
https://doi.org/10.1007/979-8-8688-0134-1

Copyright © 2024 by Farzin Asadi

Managing Director, Apress Media LLC: Welmoed Spahr
. Acquisitions Editor: Miriam Haidara
Development Editor: James Markham
Coordinating Editor: Jessica Vakili

Cover designed by eStudioCalamar

Cover image by Blue Andy (https://www.shutterstock.com/image-illustration/central-computer-processors-cpu-concept-3d-2190764501)

Distributed to the book trade worldwide by Apress Media, LLC, 1 New York Plaza, New York, NY 10004, U.S.A. Phone 1-800-SPRINGER, fax (201) 348-4505, e-mail orders-ny@springer-sbm.com, or visit www.springeronline.com. Apress Media, LLC is a California LLC and the sole member (owner) is Springer Science + Business Media Finance Inc (SSBM Finance Inc). SSBM Finance Inc is a **Delaware** corporation.

For information on translations, please e-mail booktranslations@springernature.com; for reprint, paperback, or audio rights, please e-mail bookpermissions@springernature.com.

Apress titles may be purchased in bulk for academic, corporate, or promotional use. eBook versions and licenses are also available for most titles. For more information, reference our Print and eBook Bulk Sales web page at http://www.apress.com/bulk-sales.

Any source code or other supplementary material referenced by the author in this book is available to readers on GitHub (https://github.com/Apress). For more detailed information, please visit https://www.apress.com/gp/services/source-code.

Paper in this product is recyclable

Dedicated to my dear brother, Farzad, and my lovely sisters, Farnaz and Farzaneh.

Table of Contents

About the Author

Farzin Asadi received his B.Sc. in Electronics Engineering, M.Sc. in Control Engineering, and Ph.D. in Mechatronics Engineering. Currently, he is with the Department of Electrical and Electronics Engineering at the Maltepe University, Istanbul, Turkey. Dr. Asadi has published over 40 international papers and 19 books. He is on the editorial board of seven scientific journals as well. His research interests include switching converters, control theory, robust control of power electronics converters, and robotics.

About the Technical Reviewer

Hai Van Pham received his B.Sc., M.Sc., and Ph.D. in Computer Science.

Currently he is with the School of Information and Communication Technology, Hanoi University of Science and Technology, Hanoi, Vietnam.

Dr. Pham has published over 100 papers in ISI/Scopus indexed journals. He is an associate editor in domestic and international journals and served as chair and technical committee member of many national and international conferences including SOICT 2014, KSE 2015, KSE 2017, KSE 2019, KSE 2021, and KSE 2022.

His research interests include artificial intelligence, knowledge-based systems, big data, soft computing, rule-based systems, and fuzzy systems.

Introduction

This book is just what the name implies – a simple, easy-to-follow text devoted entirely to the fundamentals of electronics. Completely avoiding unnecessary and complex technical concepts and highly mathematical terms, the subject is presented in simple language, using analogies which are familiar to everyone.

This book is written for makers and anyone who is interested in electronics engineering. After finishing the book, you will be able to read circuit schematics and implement a given circuit schematic. There are no prerequisites for reading this book.

I hope that this book will be useful to the readers, and I welcome comments on the book.

—Farzin Asadi

CHAPTER 1

Power Supply

All circuits require an energy source in order to work. The power supply (PS) is responsible for providing the required energy for the circuit. This chapter studies important power supplies.

Mains Electricity

Mains electricity or utility power, power grid, domestic power, or wall power is a general-purpose alternating current (AC) electric power supply. It is the form of electrical power that is delivered to homes and businesses through the electrical grid in many parts of the world. People use this electricity to power everyday items (such as domestic appliances, televisions and lamps) by plugging them into a wall outlet.

Waveform of mains electricity is shown in Figure 1-1. According to Figure 1-1, mains electricity has a sinusoidal waveform with peak value of Vp and period of T. In the United States, mains electricity is 120 V, 60 Hz. This means that root-mean-square (RMS) value is 120 V, peak value is $Vp = 120\sqrt{2} = 169.7\,V$, and $T = \dfrac{1}{60} = 0.0167\,s = 16.7\,ms$. Some countries use 220 V, 50 Hz. For 220 V, 50 Hz systems, root-mean-square (RMS) value is 220 V, peak value is $Vp = 220\sqrt{2} = 311.12\,V$, and $T = \dfrac{1}{50} = 0.02\,s = 20\,ms$. Schematics use the symbol shown in Figure 1-2 to show an AC source.

© Farzin Asadi 2024

F. Asadi, *ABCs of Electronics*, Maker Innovations Series,
https://doi.org/10.1007/979-8-8688-0134-1_1

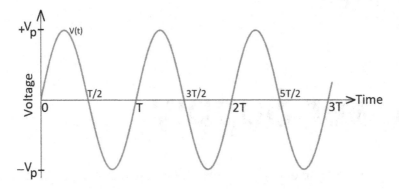

Figure 1-1. *Sinusoidal waveform* $\left(V(t)=V_p\sin(\dfrac{2\pi}{T}t)=V_p\sin(\omega t)\right)$

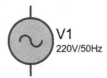

Figure 1-2. *A sinusoidal source with peak value of* $220\sqrt{2}=311.12\,V$ *and frequency of 50 Hz*

The wall outlet has three terminals: hot, neutral, and ground (Figure 1-3). The ground terminal is used for protection purposes. The hot and neutral terminals are used to transfer the energy to the consumer. Touching the hot and neutral terminals simultaneously leads to electrocution or even death.

Figure 1-3. *Wall outlet terminals*

Consider the AC consumer shown in Figure 1-4 (for instance consider an electric heater or lamp). It has two terminals: A and B. You can connect the A to the hot terminal and B to the neutral terminal, or you can connect the A to the neutral terminal and B to the hot terminal (Figure 1-5). In both cases, your device works correctly.

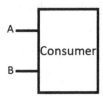

Figure 1-4. *AC load*

3

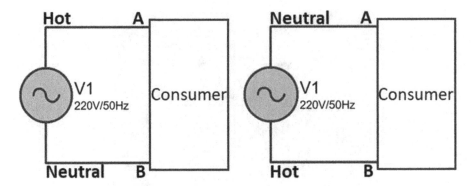

Figure 1-5. *Consumer is connected to the main*

Adaptors

Most electronic devices work with a small direct current (DC; Figure 1-6). Therefore, the mains electricity can't be given to the electronic devices directly. Mains electricity needs to be processed by a circuit and be converted into a DC voltage first. The adaptors shown in Figures 1-7, 1-8, and 1-9 convert the mains sinusoidal voltage (Figure 1-2) to a DC voltage like the one shown in Figure 1-6.

Figure 1-6. *Voltage vs. time for a 12 V DC voltage*

Figure 1-7. *A simple adaptor*

Figure 1-8. *Laptop charger*

Figure 1-9. *Cell phone charger*

The adaptors shown in Figures 1-7, 1-8 and 1-9 use two different techniques to convert the AC voltage into a DC voltage. The one shown in Figure 1-7 uses an iron core transformer. Structure of an iron core transformer is shown in Figure 1-10. It has two windings which are electrically isolated from each other. The iron core makes a path for magnetic flux generated by the primary winding. The flux passes through the secondary winding and induces a voltage in it. Peak value of induced voltage may be bigger or smaller than the primary AC voltage. Both primary and secondary windings have sinusoidal voltages.

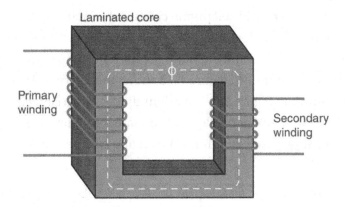

Figure 1-10. *Transformer*

When the primary winding has more turns in comparison with the secondary winding, peak value of secondary voltage is smaller than peak value of primary voltage. Such a transformer is called step-down transformer.

When the secondary winding has more turns in comparison with the primary winding, peak value of primary voltage is smaller than peak value of secondary voltage. Such a transformer is called step-up transformer. Symbols for step-down and step-up transformers are shown in Figure 1-11. Most of the electronic devices use a step-down transformer. Microwave ovens have a step-up transformer which increases the output voltage up to 1800–2800 V.

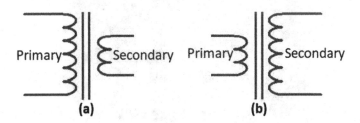

Figure 1-11. *(a) Step-down transformer. (b) Step-up transformer*

The laptop adaptor and cell phone charger shown in Figures 1-8 and 1-9 are examples of switch mode power supply (SMPS). SMPSs don't use any iron core transformer and are more complex in comparison with the adaptor shown in Figure 1-7. Figure 1-12 shows the internal circuit of the adaptor shown in Figure 1-7. It has four diodes and a capacitor only. Figure 1-13 shows an opened adaptor. Compare this figure with an opened laptop charger shown in Figure 1-14. Which one is more complex?

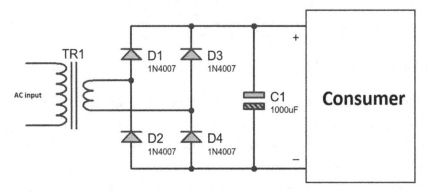

Figure 1-12. *Internal circuit for a simple adaptor*

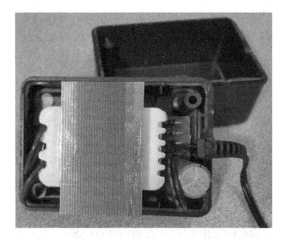

Figure 1-13. *Inside of a simple adaptor*

Figure 1-14. *Inside of a laptop charger*

Laboratory Power Supplies

Laboratory power supplies are used to test the circuits in laboratory environment. They are connected to the mains electricity and generate the desired DC voltage in the output. Standard laboratory power supplies can generate 0–30 V with maximum output current of 3 A. A sample of a laboratory power supply is shown in Figure 1-15.

Figure 1-15. *Laboratory power supply*

9

The laboratory power supply shown in Figure 1-15 is a two channel power supply. Two channel power supplies have two outputs and each output can be set independently. A two channel power supply is more expensive than a single output power supply.

The output current of the laboratory power is adjustable and can be limited by the user. By setting the current limit, the damages caused by shorts and overcurrents can be prevented.

Batteries

Batteries are devices that convert chemical energy into electric energy. Some commonly used batteries are shown in Figures 1-16 and 1-17.

Figure 1-16. *1.5 V and 9 V batteries*

Figure 1-17. *Car battery*

Batteries generate DC voltages. For instance, voltage waveform of a 9 V battery is shown in Figure 1-18. Figure 1-19 shows the symbol of battery in schematics.

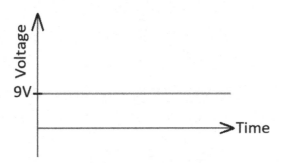

Figure 1-18. *Voltage vs. time for a battery*

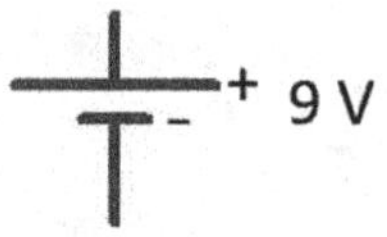

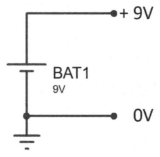

Figure 1-19. *Symbol of battery*

Each battery has two terminals. One of the terminals has a + label and the other one has a – label. We assume that current goes from positive terminal toward the negative terminal. The + terminal has a higher potential in comparison with the – terminal. For instance, for a 9 V battery, $V_{positive\ terminal} - V_{negative\ terminal} = 9\ V$.

The ground symbol shown in Figure 1-20 is used to determine the node/nodes with zero potential. For instance, in Figure 1-21, the ground symbol is connected to the negative terminal of the battery. This means that negative terminal of the battery is considered as potential reference. Note that the ground symbol shown in Figure 1-21 shows the reference of potential only and there is no physical connection between the negative terminal of the battery and something else.

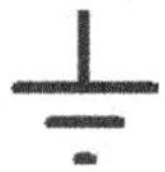

Figure 1-20. *Ground symbol*

Figure 1-21. *Negative terminal is selected as ground*

You can take the positive terminal of the battery as potential reference as well (Figure 1-22). However, this selection is not a widely used one. The commonly used selection is the one shown in Figure 1-21.

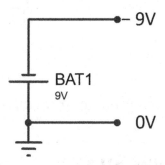

Figure 1-22. *Positive terminal is selected as ground*

Consider the circuit shown in Figure 1-23. In this circuit, three series resistors are connected to a 9 V battery. The schematics shown in Figures 1-24 and 1-25 are equivalent to Figure 1-23.

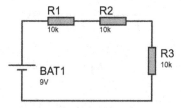

Figure 1-23. *A simple circuit*

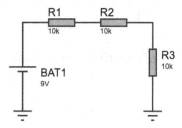

Figure 1-24. *Equivalent schematic for circuit shown in Figure 1-23*

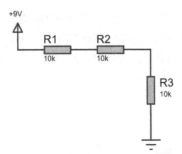

Figure 1-25. *Equivalent schematic for circuit shown in Figure 1-23*

Symmetric Power Supply

Sometimes your circuit requires both positive and negative voltages (Op Amp ICs generally require symmetric voltages). You can use two batteries to make a symmetric power supply. For instance, in Figure 1-26, two batteries are used to make -9 V, 0 V, and +9 V.

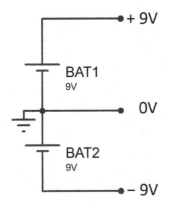

Figure 1-26. *Generation of positive and negative voltages with two batteries*

Inverter

In the previous sections, you learned that adaptors convert AC into DC. Is it possible to convert DC into AC as well? The answer for this question is "yes." A device called inverter can be used to convert DC into AC (Figure 1-27). Inverters can be used to make AC electric from the DC voltage generated by the solar panels.

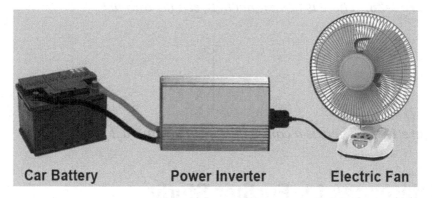

Car Battery   **Power Inverter**   **Electric Fan**

Figure 1-27. Inverter converts a DC voltage into an AC voltage

Inverters make the heart of an uninterruptable power supply (UPS) as well. UPS is a device that allows a computer to keep running for at least a short time when incoming power is interrupted. Such a short time permits you to save your work and at least avoid data loss.

Conventions Used in This Book

In this book the symbols shown in Figure 1-28 are used to show pass of two wires over each other without any connection. Figure 1-29 shows two wires are connected to each other.

15

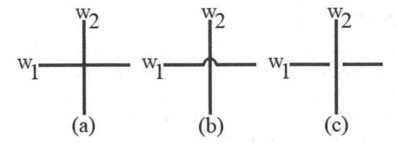

Figure 1-28. *There is no contact between w1 and w2*

Figure 1-29. *There is a contact between w1 and w2*

References for Further Study

[1] Asadi F., Analog Electronic Circuits Laboratory Manual, Springer, 2023. DOI: https://doi.org/10.1007/978-3-031-25122-1

[2] Asadi F., Digital Circuits Laboratory Manual, Springer, 2023. DOI: https://doi.org/10.1007/978-3-031-41516-6

[3] Asadi F., Electric Circuits Laboratory Manual, Springer, 2023. DOI: https://doi.org/10.1007/978-3-031-24552-7

[4] Asadi F., Eguchi K., Electronic Measurement: A Practical Approach, Springer, 2021. DOI: https://doi.org/10.1007/978-3-031-02021-6

[5] Asadi F., Essential Circuit Analysis using NI Multisim™ and MATLAB®, Springer, 2022. DOI: https://doi.org/10.1007/978-3-030-89850-2

[6] Asadi F., Essential Circuit Analysis Using Proteus®, Springer, 2022. DOI: https://doi.org/10.1007/978-981-19-4353-9

[7] Asadi F., Essential Circuit Analysis using LTspice®, Springer, 2022. DOI: https://doi.org/10.1007/978-3-031-09853-6

[8]   Asadi F., Electric and Electronic Circuit Simulation using TINA-TI®, River Publishers, 2022. DOI: https://doi.org/10.13052/rp-9788770226851

[9]   Asadi F., Electric Circuit Analysis with EasyEDA, Springer, 2022. DOI: https://doi.org/10.1007/978-3-031-00292-2

[10] Asadi F., Power Electronics Circuit Analysis with PSIM®, De Gruyter, 2021. DOI: https://doi.org/10.1515/9783110740653

[11] Asadi F., Simulation of Power Electronics Circuits with MATLAB®/Simulink®: Design, Analyze, and Prototype Power Electronics, Apress, 2022. DOI: https://doi.org/10.1007/978-1-4842-8220-5

[12] Asadi F., Eguchi K., Simulation of Power Electronics Converters Using PLECS®, Academic Press, 2019. DOI: https://doi.org/10.1016/C2018-0-02253-7

CHAPTER 2

Mechanical Switches

In electrical engineering, a switch is an electrical component that can disconnect or connect the conducting path in an electrical circuit, interrupting the electric current or diverting it from one conductor to another.

The most common type of switch is a mechanical device consisting of one or more sets of movable electrical contacts connected to external circuits. When a pair of contacts is touching, current can pass between them, while when the contacts are separated, no current can flow. This chapter introduces the most commonly used mechanical switches.

Single Pole Single Throw (SPST) Switch

A single pole single throw (SPST) switch is shown in Figure 2-1. SPST has only two terminals. The symbol of SPST is shown in Figure 2-2.

Figure 2-1. *An SPST switch*

© Farzin Asadi 2024
F. Asadi, *ABCs of Electronics*, Maker Innovations Series,
https://doi.org/10.1007/979-8-8688-0134-1_2

Figure 2-2. *Symbol for SPST switch*

The switch shown in Figure 2-2 is an open switch. Therefore, the current cannot pass through it. The switch shown in Figure 2-3 is closed and the current can pass through it.

Figure 2-3. *Closed SPST switch*

Let's study an example. Figure 2-4 shows the circuit that you use in your home to turn on/off a light bulb. The AC source shows the main. When you close the switch, the lamp turns on since the current passes through it (Figure 2-5).

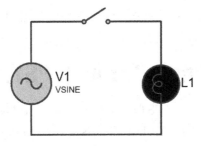

Figure 2-4. *A simple circuit*

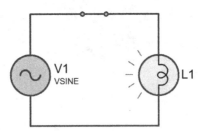

Figure 2-5. *Lamp turns on when the switch is closed*

Single Pole Double Throw (SPDT) Switches

Two single pole double throw (SPDT) switches are shown in Figure 2-6.

Figure 2-6. *SPDT switches*

SPDT has three terminals. In one state, the common terminal C is connected to the terminal X (Figure 2-7). In the other state, the common terminal C is connected to the terminal Y (Figure 2-8).

Figure 2-7. *Common terminal is connected to X*

Figure 2-8. *Common terminal is connected to Y*

Let's study an example. Consider the circuit shown in Figure 2-9. This circuit is used to control the lamp of corridors (Figure 2-9 used a battery but in real corridors, mains electricity is used). In Figure 2-9, the SPDT A and B are installed in two different locations, generally two ends of the corridor. This circuit permits you to control a lamp with two switches. You can turn the lamp on/off with any of the switches.

21

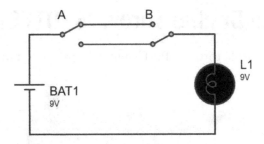

Figure 2-9. *Control of one light bulb from two different locations*

In Figure 2-9, the lamp is off since there is no path for current flow. Now assume that you are in the B location and you have access to SPDT B and you need to turn on the lamp. In this case, you press the SPDT B and the lamp turns on (Figure 2-10).

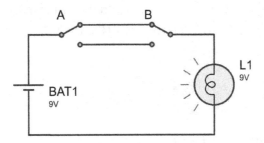

Figure 2-10. *Lamp is on*

In Figure 2-10, the lamp is on since there is a path for current flow. Now assume that you are in the A location and you have access to SPDT A and you need to turn off the lamp. In this case, you press the SPDT A and the lamp turns off (Figure 2-11).

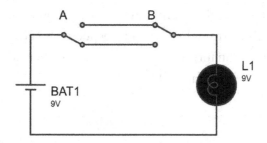

Figure 2-11. *Lamp is off*

Make the circuit shown in Figure 2-9 and test it. Ensure that you can turn the lamp on/off with any of the switches.

Double Pole Double Throw (DPDT) Switches

A double pole double throw (DPDT) switch is shown in Figure 2-12.

Figure 2-12. *DPDT switch*

DPDT has six terminals. In one state, the common terminal C1 and C2 are connected to the terminal X1 and Y1, respectively (Figure 2-13). In the other state, the common terminal C1 and C2 are connected to the terminal X2 and Y2, respectively (Figure 2-14).

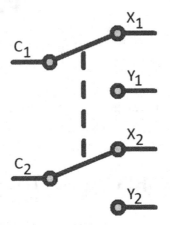

Figure 2-13. *C1 and C2 are connected to X1 and X2, respectively*

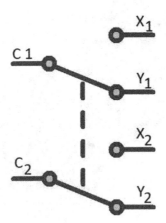

Figure 2-14. *C1 and C2 are connected to Y1 and Y2, respectively*

One of the DPDT applications is shown in Section 11.3 of Chapter 11.

Push Buttons

A push button switch (Figure 2-15) causes a temporary change in an electrical circuit only while the switch is physically pushed. A spring returns the switch to its original position immediately afterward. For instance, push buttons are used in door bells. When you push the button, the doorbell rings. When you release the push button, it stops. Push buttons are used in door bells, remote controls, calculators, and cars as well (Figures 2-16, 2-17, 2-18, and 2-19).

Figure 2-15. *Push button*

Figure 2-16. *Door bell is activated by a push button*

Figure 2-17. *Remote controls have several push buttons*

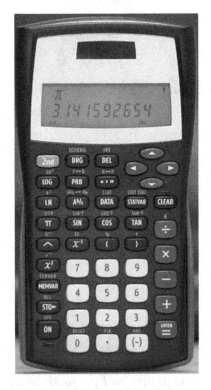

Figure 2-18. *Calculators have several push buttons*

Figure 2-19. *Car horn is activated by a push button*

The push button symbol is shown in Figure 2-20.

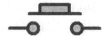

Figure 2-20. *Push button symbol*

References for Further Study

[1] Asadi F., Analog Electronic Circuits Laboratory Manual, Springer, 2023. DOI: https://doi.org/10.1007/978-3-031-25122-1

[2] Asadi F., Digital Circuits Laboratory Manual, Springer, 2023. DOI: https://doi.org/10.1007/978-3-031-41516-6

[3] Asadi F., Electric Circuits Laboratory Manual, Springer, 2023. DOI: https://doi.org/10.1007/978-3-031-24552-7

[4] Asadi F., Eguchi K., Electronic Measurement: A Practical Approach, Springer, 2021. DOI: https://doi.org/10.1007/978-3-031-02021-6

[5] Asadi F., Essential Circuit Analysis using NI Multisim™ and MATLAB®, Springer, 2022. DOI: https://doi.org/10.1007/978-3-030-89850-2

[6] Asadi F., Essential Circuit Analysis Using Proteus®, Springer, 2022. DOI: https://doi.org/10.1007/978-981-19-4353-9

[7]   Asadi F., Essential Circuit Analysis using LTspice®, Springer, 2022. DOI: https://doi.org/10.1007/978-3-031-09853-6

[8]   Asadi F., Electric and Electronic Circuit Simulation using TINA-TI®, River Publishers, 2022. DOI: https://doi.org/10.13052/rp-9788770226851

[9]   Asadi F., Electric Circuit Analysis with EasyEDA, Springer, 2022. DOI: https://doi.org/10.1007/978-3-031-00292-2

[10] Asadi F., Power Electronics Circuit Analysis with PSIM®, De Gruyter, 2021. DOI: https://doi.org/10.1515/9783110740653

[11] Asadi F., Simulation of Power Electronics Circuits with MATLAB®/Simulink®: Design, Analyze, and Prototype Power Electronics, Apress, 2022. DOI: https://doi.org/10.1007/978-1-4842-8220-5

[12] Asadi F., Eguchi K., Simulation of Power Electronics Converters Using PLECS®, Academic Press, 2019. DOI: https://doi.org/10.1016/C2018-0-02253-7

CHAPTER 3

Capacitors and Inductors

Capacitors and inductors are important parts of electronic circuits. Both of them are energy storage devices. Capacitors store the energy in the electric field, while inductors store energy in the magnetic field.

This chapter studies the capacitors and inductors.

Capacitors

A capacitor is a device that stores electrical energy in an electric field by accumulating electric charges on two closely spaced surfaces that are insulated from each other. Figure 3-1 shows inside of a capacitor.

© Farzin Asadi 2024
F. Asadi, *ABCs of Electronics*, Maker Innovations Series,
https://doi.org/10.1007/979-8-8688-0134-1_3

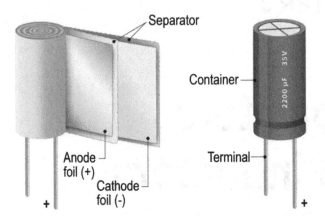

Figure 3-1. *Structure of a capacitor*

The unit of capacitance is farad (abbreviated F), named after Michael Faraday. For most applications, the farad is an impractically large unit of capacitance. Most electrical and electronic applications are covered by the following SI prefixes:

1 mF (millifarad, one thousandth (10^{-3}) of a farad)
= 0.001 F = 1000 µF = 1000000000 pF

1 µF (microfarad, one millionth (10^{-6}) of a farad)
= 0.000 001 F = 1000 nF = 1000000 pF

1 nF (nanofarad, one billionth (10^{-9}) of a farad)
= 0.000 000 001 F = 0.001 µF = 1000 pF

1 pF (picofarad, one trillionth (10^{-12}) of a farad)
= 0.000 000 000 001 F = 0.001 nF

Some of the commonly used capacitors are shown in Figures 3-2, 3-3, and 3-4.

Figure 3-2. Electrolytic capacitor

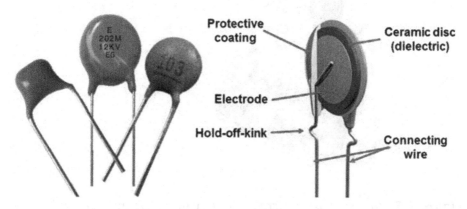

Figure 3-3. Ceramic capacitors

Figure 3-4. Variable capacitors

Electrolytic capacitors (Figure 3-5) are used when there is a requirement for large capacitance. Electrolytic capacitors are polarized components. This means that reverse voltage can destroy them.

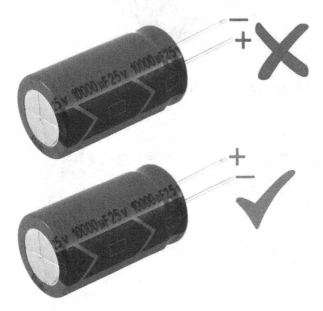

Figure 3-5. *Incorrect and correct polarity for electrolytic capacitors*

Ceramic capacitors are non-polarized capacitors. Therefore, the polarity of applied voltage is not important (Figure 3-6).

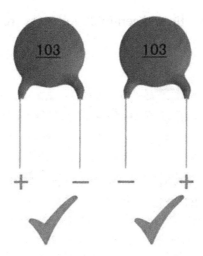

Figure 3-6. *Ceramic capacitors are not sensitive to voltage polarity*

SMD capacitor (Figure 3-7) is nothing but a capacitor with compact size and no long lead. The size of the surface mount capacitor is smaller than the traditional capacitor space, and the device can be confined in a smaller area, useful in portable devices. Some of the SMD capacitors are polarized.

Figure 3-7. *SMD capacitors*

Symbols for electrolytic and ceramic capacitors are shown in Figure 3-8.

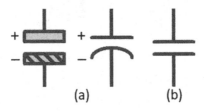

(a)   (b)

Figure 3-8. *Commonly used symbols for (a) electrolytic capacitors and (b) ceramic capacitors*

Values of Capacitor

In electrolytic capacitors, capacitance and working voltage of the capacitor are printed on the capacitor. For instance, a 3300 µF capacitor with working voltage of 35 V is shown in Figure 3-9. Working voltage is the maximum voltage at which the capacitor operates without leaking excessively or arcing through.

Figure 3-9. *An electrolytic capacitor with working voltage of 35 V*

Ceramic capacitors are quite small, and it is not possible to print the capacitance on the capacitor. Ceramic capacitors usually uses three digits like 102, 103, or 101 for indicating their values, and the values are in terms of picofarad. If a ceramic capacitor has three digits,

ABC, then the value would be $AB \times 10^C$ picofarad. For instance, in Figure 3-10, 104 is printed on the capacitor. Therefore, the capacitance is $10 \times 10^4 = 100000\ pF = 100\ nF$. Note that $1000\ pF = 1\ nF$ and $1000\ nF = 1\ \mu F$.

Figure 3-10. *A ceramic capacitor with capacitance of 100 nF*

Figure 3-11 shows a capacitor with value of $47 \times 10^5 = 4700000\ pF = 4700\ nF = 4.7\ uF$.

Figure 3-11. *A ceramic capacitor with capacitance of 4.7 μF*

35

Series and Parallel Connection of Capacitors

Series connection of two capacitors is shown in Figure 3-12. For series connection, the equivalent capacitance between points A and B is $\dfrac{C1\times C2}{C1+C2}$.

For instance, equivalent capacitance for series connection of two 10 µF capacitors is $\dfrac{10\ \mu F\times 10\ \mu F}{10\ \mu F+10\ \mu F}=5\ \mu F$.

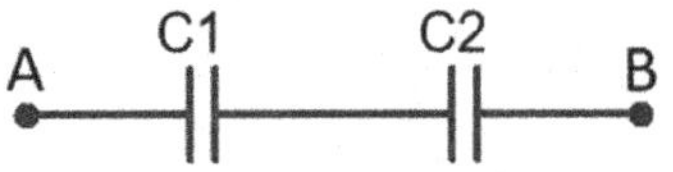

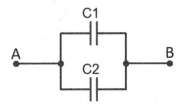

Figure 3-12. *Series connected capacitors*

Parallel connection of two capacitors is shown in Figure 3-13. For parallel connection, the equivalent capacitance between points A and B is C1+C2. For instance, equivalent capacitance for parallel connection of two 10 µF capacitors is $10\ \mu F+10\ \mu F=20\ \mu F$.

Figure 3-13. *Parallel connected capacitors*

Charging a Capacitor

Consider the circuit shown in Figure 3-14. Initial voltage of the capacitor is zero. When you close the switch, the capacitor starts to charge, and after $5\times R_1\times C_1$, it will reach the its final value which is battery voltage.

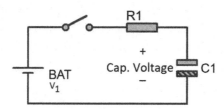

Figure 3-14. *A simple circuit to charge a capacitor*

For instance, when you close the switch in Figure 3-15, the voltage goes from 0 *V* to 9 *V* within $5 \times 1k \times 1000\ \mu F = 5\ s$. Graph of capacitor voltage is shown in Figure 3-16.

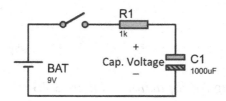

Figure 3-15. *Circuit of Figure 3-14 with R1=1 kΩ and C1=1000 μF*

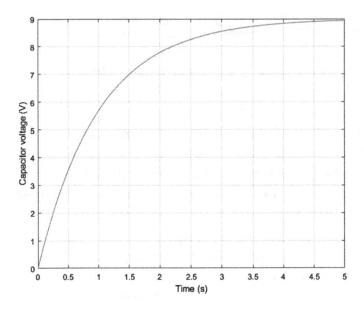

Figure 3-16. *Voltage of capacitor in Figure 3-15*

Discharging a Capacitor

Assume that you have a charged capacitor (Figure 3-17). The capacitor
starts to discharge if you connect the capacitor to a resistor (Figure 3-18).
The discharge process requires $5 \times R \times C$ seconds.

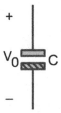

Figure 3-17. *A charged capacitor*

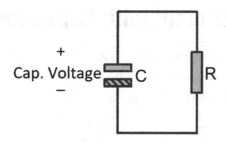

Figure 3-18. *A simple discharge circuit*

For instance, assume that $V_0 = 9$ V, $R = 1$ $k\Omega$, and $C = 1000$ μF. In this case, the discharge process takes 5 s. Graph of capacitor voltage is shown in Figure 3-19.

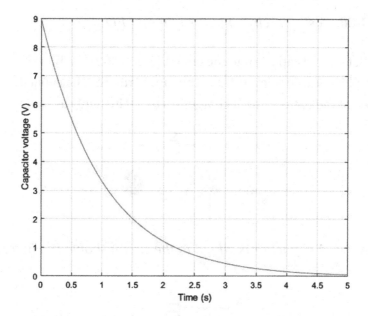

Figure 3-19. *Voltage of capacitor in Figure 3-18 ($V_0 = 9$ V, $R = 1$ $k\Omega$, and $C = 1000$ μF)*

Simple Experiment with Capacitor

Consider the circuit shown in Figure 3-20. When you press the push button, the LED turns on and when you release the push button, the LED turns off. LEDs are studied in Chapter 5.

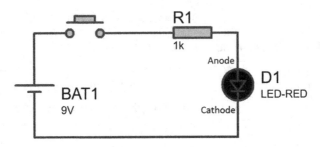

Figure 3-20. *A simple circuit to turn on an LED*

Now let's add a capacitor to the circuit (Figure 3-21). When you press the push button (Figure 3-22), the LED turns on. The capacitor is connected to the battery and it charges up to 9 V instantly as well.

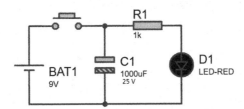

Figure 3-21. *A capacitor is added to the circuit shown in Figure 3-20*

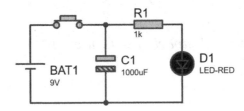

Figure 3-22. *Push button is pressed and capacitor is charged*

Now release the push button (Figure 3-23). The LED remains on although there is no connection between the LED and battery. The LED remains on until the capacitor C1 discharges. This shows the energy storage capability of the capacitor.

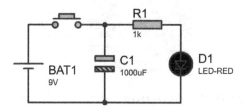

Figure 3-23. *Push button is released but the LED remains on for a while*

Inductors

An inductor, is a two-terminal electrical component that stores energy in a magnetic field when electric current flows through it. An inductor typically consists of an insulated wire wound around a core (Figures 3-24 and 3-25). Sometimes the inductor has no core (Figure 3-26).

Figure 3-24. *An inductor with ferrite core*

41

Figure 3-25. *An inductor with iron core*

Figure 3-26. *Air core inductors*

The unit of inductance is henry (abbreviated H), named after Joseph Henry. For most applications, the henry is an impractically large unit of inductance. Most electrical and electronic applications are covered by the following SI prefixes:

1 mH (millihenry, one thousandth (10^{-3}) of a henry)
= 0.001 H = 1000 µH

1 µH (microhenry, one millionth (10^{-6}) of a henry)
= 0.000001 F

The symbol of inductor is shown in Figure 3-27.

Figure 3-27. *Symbol of inductor*

Series and Parallel Connection of Inductors

Series connection of two inductors is shown in Figure 3-28. For series connection, the equivalent inductance between points A and B is $L_1 + L_2$. For instance, equivalent inductance for series connection of two 10 μH inductors is 20 μH.

Figure 3-28. *Series connected inductors*

Parallel connection of two inductors is shown in Figure 3-29. For parallel connection, the equivalent inductance between points A and B is $\dfrac{L_1 \times L_2}{L_1 + L_2}$. For instance, equivalent inductance for parallel connection of two 10 μH inductors is $\dfrac{10\ \mu H \times 10\ \mu H}{10\ \mu H + 10\ \mu H} = 5\ \mu H$.

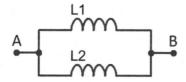

Figure 3-29. *Parallel connected inductors*

Inductors in DC Circuits

Let's see the behavior of inductors in DC circuits. Consider the circuit shown in Figure 3-30. At t=0, the switch is closed. The circuit current for [0, 6 µs] interval is shown in Figure 3-31. According to Ohm's law, the current is $\dfrac{9}{100} = 0.09\ A$.

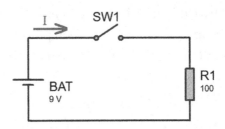

Figure 3-30. *A simple circuit*

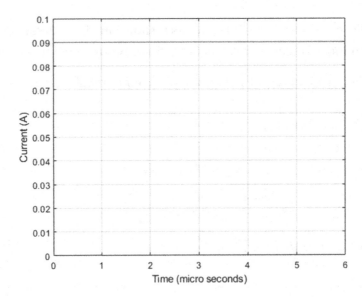

Figure 3-31. *Current graph for circuit shown in Figure 3-30*

Now assume that a 100 µH inductor is added to the circuit
(Figure 3-32). The switch is closed at t=0. The circuit current for [0, 6 µs]
interval is shown in Figure 3-33. The current goes toward 0.09 A but it
took around 5 µs to reach the final value. In other words, the presence of
inductor slows down the current. The capacitor slows down the voltage
(Figure 3-16).

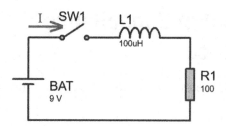

Figure 3-32. *A 100 µH inductor is added to the circuit shown in*
Figure 3-30

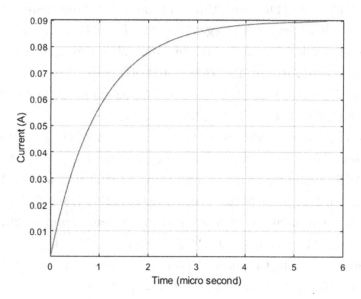

Figure 3-33. *Current graph for circuit shown in Figure 3-32*

45

Applications of Inductors

Inductors play an important role in electronic circuits. For instance, they are used as filters (a circuit that separates some frequencies from others), tuning circuits, electric motors, transformers, etc.

Measurement of Capacitance and Inductance

You can use an "RLC meter" to measure the capacitance and inductance.

References for Further Study

[1]   Asadi F., Analog Electronic Circuits Laboratory Manual, Springer, 2023. DOI: https://doi.org/10.1007/978-3-031-25122-1

[2]   Asadi F., Digital Circuits Laboratory Manual, Springer, 2023. DOI: https://doi.org/10.1007/978-3-031-41516-6

[3]   Asadi F., Electric Circuits Laboratory Manual, Springer, 2023. DOI: https://doi.org/10.1007/978-3-031-24552-7

[4]   Asadi F., Eguchi K., Electronic Measurement: A Practical Approach, Springer, 2021. DOI: https://doi.org/10.1007/978-3-031-02021-6

[5]   Asadi F., Essential Circuit Analysis using NI Multisim™ and MATLAB®, Springer, 2022. DOI: https://doi.org/10.1007/978-3-030-89850-2

[6]   Asadi F., Essential Circuit Analysis Using Proteus®, Springer, 2022. DOI: https://doi.org/10.1007/978-981-19-4353-9

[7]   Asadi F., Essential Circuit Analysis using LTspice®, Springer, 2022. DOI: https://doi.org/10.1007/978-3-031-09853-6

[8]   Asadi F., Electric and Electronic Circuit Simulation using TINA-TI®, River Publishers, 2022. DOI: https://doi.org/10.13052/rp-9788770226851

[9]   Asadi F., Electric Circuit Analysis with EasyEDA, Springer, 2022. DOI: https://doi.org/10.1007/978-3-031-00292-2

[10]   Asadi F., Power Electronics Circuit Analysis with PSIM®, De Gruyter, 2021. DOI: https://doi.org/10.1515/9783110740653

[11]   Asadi F., Simulation of Power Electronics Circuits with MATLAB®/ Simulink®: Design, Analyze, and Prototype Power Electronics, Apress, 2022. DOI: https://doi.org/10.1007/978-1-4842-8220-5

[12]   Asadi F., Eguchi K., Simulation of Power Electronics Converters Using PLECS®, Academic Press, 2019. DOI: https://doi.org/10.1016/C2018-0-02253-7

CHAPTER 4

Resistors

A resistor (Figure 4-1) is a two-terminal electrical component that implements electrical resistance as a circuit element. In electronic circuits, resistors are used to reduce current flow, adjust signal levels, divide voltages, bias active elements, and terminate transmission lines, among other uses.

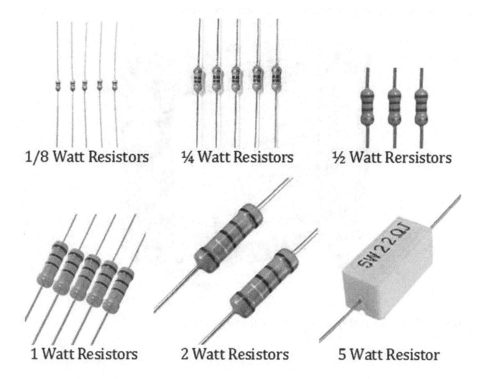

1/8 Watt Resistors   ¼ Watt Resistors   ½ Watt Rersistors

1 Watt Resistors   2 Watt Resistors   5 Watt Resistor

Figure 4-1. *Different resistors with different wattages*

© Farzin Asadi 2024
F. Asadi, *ABCs of Electronics*, Maker Innovations Series,
https://doi.org/10.1007/979-8-8688-0134-1_4

Commonly used symbols for resistors are shown in Figure 4-2.

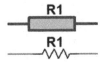

Figure 4-2. *Symbol of resistor*

The unit of electrical resistance is Ohms and it is shown with Ω. For instance, 1 kΩ and 1 MΩ show 1 kilo Ohm and 1 mega Ohm, respectively (note that 1 kΩ = 1000 Ω and 1 MΩ = 1000000 Ω).

Resistors dissipate power as heat when current passes through them (Figure 4-3). The power rating of a resistor is measured in Watts. For instance, a 2 W resistor can dissipate up to 2 W safely. Price of the resistor (and its dimension) increases as its wattage increases.

Figure 4-3. *A heater is a high power resistor*

Ohm's Law

Ohm's law states that the voltage across a conductor is directly proportional to the current flowing through it, provided all physical conditions and temperatures remain constant. Mathematically, this current-voltage relationship is written as $V = R \times I$ (Figure 4-4). In this equation, the constant of proportionality, R, is called resistance and has units of Ohms, with the symbol Ω.

Figure 4-4. *Parameters of Ohm's law*

Ohm's law is an empirical relation which accurately describes the conductivity of the vast majority of electrically conductive materials over many orders of magnitude of current. However, some materials do not obey Ohm's law; these are called nonohmic.

Power Dissipated in Resistors

Assume that you connected a resistor to a battery (Figure 4-5). In this case, power dissipated in the resistor is $P_{dissipated} = \dfrac{V_{battery}^2}{R}$. For instance, if you connect a 100 Ω resistor to a 9 V battery, dissipated power will be

$$P_{dissipated} = \frac{V_{battery}^2}{R} = \frac{9^2}{100} = 0.81\,W = 810\,mW.$$ Note that mW shows milliwatt.

$1\,mW = 0.001\,W$. 810 mW of power means that the resistor dissipated 810 milli Joule in 1 second. According to Ohm's law, the current in the 100 Ω resistor is I=V/R=9/100=0.09 A or 90 mA.

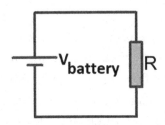

Figure 4-5. *A resistor is connected to a battery*

Now consider the circuit shown in Figure 4-6. In this case, a resistor is connected to an AC source which has a sinusoidal voltage with peak value of V_p volts (Figure 4-7). In this case, average power dissipated in the resistor is $P_{dissipated} = \dfrac{V_p^{\,2}}{2R}$. For instance, if you connect a 100 Ω resistor to a sinusoidal voltage with peak value of $V_p = 9\ V$, dissipated average power will be $P_{dissipated} = \dfrac{V_p^{\,2}}{2R} = \dfrac{9^2}{2 \times 100} = 0.405\,W = 405\,mW.$

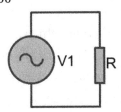

Figure 4-6. *A resistor is connected to a sinusoidal voltage source*

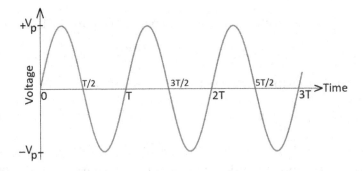

Figure 4-7. *Sinusoidal waveform*

The equation of the waveform shown in Figure 4-7 is $V = V_p \sin\left(\dfrac{2\pi}{T}t\right)$.

Therefore, according to the Ohm's law, the current that passes through the resistor shown in Figure 4-7 is $I = \dfrac{V}{R} = \dfrac{V_p \sin\left(\dfrac{2\pi}{T}t\right)}{R} = \dfrac{V_p}{R}\sin\left(\dfrac{2\pi}{T}t\right)$.

Series and Parallel Resistors

Series connection of two resistors is shown in Figure 4-8. Equivalent resistance between A and B is R1+R2. For instance, series connection of a 1 kΩ resistor with a 470 Ω resistor is R1+R2=1000+470=1470 Ω.

A R1   R2   B

Figure 4-8. *Series connected resistors*

Parallel connection of two resistors is shown in Figure 4-9. Equivalent resistance between A and B is $\dfrac{R1 \times R2}{R1 + R2}$. For instance, parallel connection of a 1 kΩ resistor with a 470 Ω resistor is $\dfrac{R1 \times R2}{R1 + R2} = \dfrac{1000 \times 470}{1000 + 470} = 319.73\,\Omega$.

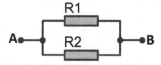

Figure 4-9. *Parallel connected resistors*

The series combination of two resistances is always greater than either individual resistance. The parallel combination of two resistances is always less than resistance of either individual resistance.

Tolerance of Resistors

Any component used in a circuit has a tolerance. The tolerance of a component is a measure of accuracy and indicates how much the measured actual value is different from its nominal expected value. For instance, a resistor with nominal value of 1 kΩ and tolerance of 5% may have any value between 1 kΩ×0.95=0.95 kΩ and 1 kΩ×1.05=1.05 kΩ.

Value of Resistors

Using color bands (Figure 4-10) is a commonly employed method to show the value of resistors. This method is used for small non-bulky resistors. The number of color bands may be 4 or 5 (four-band resistors are the most commonly used type).

In resistors with four color bands, three bands show the value of resistor and one band shows the tolerance.

In resistors with five color bands, four bands show the value of resistor and one band shows the tolerance.

Figure 4-10. *Value of resistor is shown with color bands*

Values associated with each color code is shown in Table 4-1. It is a good idea to memorize this table.

Table 4-1. *Digits associated with colors*

Color	Digit associated with the color
Black	0
Brown	1
Red	2
Orange	3
Yellow	4
Green	5
Blue	6
Violet	7
Gray	8
White	9

In resistors with four color bands, the first and second color bands show the first and second digits, and the third color band shows the multiplier. The fourth color band shows the tolerance and usually takes the colors shown in Table 4-2. For instance, assume that the third band is green. In this case, the first two digits must be multiplied with $10^5 = 100000$. Note that when third color is gold, the first two digits must be divided by 10.

Table 4-2. *Tolerance associated with colors*

Color	Tolerance associated with the color
Golden	5%
Silver	10%

For instance, a resistor with brown-green-red-gold color bands shows a $15 \times 10^2 = 15 \times 100 = 1500\ \Omega = 1.5\ k\Omega$ resistor with tolerance of 5%. The actual value of such a resistor can take any value from $1.5\ k\Omega \times 0.95 = 1.43\ k\Omega$ to $1.5\ k\Omega \times 1.05 = 1.58\ k\Omega$.

Table 4-3 shows color bands of different resistors. In this table, for instance, 5R6 shows 5.6 Ω, 8K2 shows 8.2 kΩ, 330K shows 330 kΩ, 12M shows 12 MΩ, and 3M9 shows 3.9 MΩ.

Table 4-3. *Color bands for different resistors*

		Band 3							
Band 1	Band 2	Gold	Black	Brown	Red	Orange	Yellow	Green	Blue
Brown	Black	1R0	10R	100R	1K0	10K	100K	1M0	10M
Brown	Red	1R2	12R	120R	1K2	12K	120K	1M2	12M
Brown	Green	1R5	15R	150R	1K5	15K	150K	1M5	15M
Brown	Grey	1R8	18R	180R	1K8	18K	180K	1M8	18M
Red	Red	2R2	22R	220R	2K2	22K	220K	2M2	22M
Red	Violet	2R7	27R	270R	2K7	27K	270K	2M7	27M
Orange	Orange	3R3	33R	330R	3K3	33K	330K	3M3	33M
Orange	White	3R9	39R	390R	3K9	39K	390K	3M9	39M
Yellow	Violet	4R7	47R	470R	4K7	47K	470K	4M7	47M
Green	Blue	5R6	56R	560R	5K6	56K	560K	5M6	56M
Blue	Grey	6R8	68R	680R	6K8	68K	680K	6M8	68M
Grey	Red	8R2	82R	820R	8K2	82K	820K	8M2	82M

In resistors with five color bands (Figure 4-11), the first, second, and third color bands show the first, second, and third digits, and the fourth color band shows the multiplier. The fifth color band shows the tolerance and usually takes the colors shown in Table 4-4. Note that when the fourth color is gold, the first three digits must be divided by 10. For instance, green-brown-black-red-brown (Figure 4-11) shows 51 kΩ with tolerance of 1%. Minimum and maximum values of this resistor are 50.49 kΩ and 51.51 Ω.

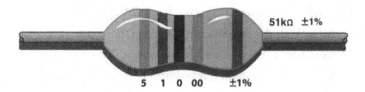

Figure 4-11. *Resistor with five color bands*

Table 4-4. *Tolerance associated with colors*

Color	Tolerance associated with the color
Brown	1%
Red	2%
Golden	5%
Silver	10%

A logical question is "How do I know which end of the resistor to start reading from?". The following clues help you to find answer for this question:

A) Many resistors have some of the color bands grouped closer together or grouped toward one end. Hold the resistor with these grouped bands to your left. Always read resistors from left to right.

B) Resistors never start with a metallic band on the left. If you have a resistor with a gold or silver band on one end, you have a 5% or 10% tolerance resistor. Position the resistor with this band on the right side, and again read your resistor from left to right.

C) Basic resistor values range from 0.1 Ω to 10
MΩ. With that knowledge, realize that on a
four-band resistor, the third color will always be
blue or less and on a five-band resistor, the fourth
color will always be green or less.

In big bulky resistors, there is enough space to write the nominal value
and tolerance code using numbers and alphabet letters. For instance, the
resistor shown in Figure 4-12 has nominal value of 0.47 Ω and is capable
to dissipate 5 W of heat. According to Table 4-5, letter J shows that this
resistor has tolerance of 5%. Therefore, the actual value of the resistor may
be between 0.95×0.47 Ω= 0.45 Ω and 1.05×0.47 Ω=0.49 Ω.

Figure 4-12. *Resistance and tolerance are written on the*
resistor body

Table 4-5. *Tolerance associated with letters*

Letter	Tolerance associated with the letter
B	0.1%
C	0.25%
D	0.5%
F	1%
G	2%
J	5%
K	10%
M	20%

The standard resistor values are organized into a set of series of values known as the E-series. E24 series is the most commonly used series. In E24 series, all of the values shown in Table 4-6 multiplied by 10^n where $-1 \leq n \leq 6$ are available. For instance, 0.27 Ω, 2.7 Ω, 27 Ω, 270 Ω, 2.7 kΩ, 27 kΩ, 270 kΩ, and 2.7 MΩ are available in this series. Tolerance of E24 series is 5%.

Table 4-6. *E24 standard resistor series*

1.0	1.1	1.2
1.3	1.5	1.6
1.8	2.0	2.2
2.4	2.7	3.0
3.3	3.6	3.9
4.3	4.7	5.1
5.6	6.2	6.8
7.5	8.2	9.1

Potentiometer

A potentiometer is a manually adjustable variable resistor with three terminals (Figure 4-13). Two of the terminals are connected to the opposite ends of a resistive element, and the third terminal connects to a sliding contact, called a wiper, moving over the (uniform) resistive element. The potentiometer essentially functions as a variable resistance divider. The resistive element can be seen as two resistors in series (the total potentiometer resistance), where the wiper position determines the resistance ratio of the first resistor to the second resistor.

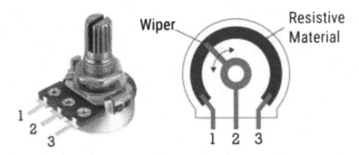

Figure 4-13. *A real potentiometer and its structure*

Commonly used symbol for potentiometer is shown in Figure 4-14.

Figure 4-14. *Potentiometer symbol*

Potentiometers are commonly used to control values in audio and video devices or systems, including volume, brightness, contrast, and color (Figure 4-15).

Figure 4-15. *Potentiometers are widely used in audio and video devices*

You can make a variable resistor with the aid of connections shown in Figures 4-16 and 4-17.

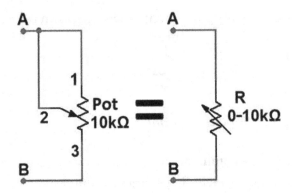

Figure 4-16. *First method to make a variable resistor*

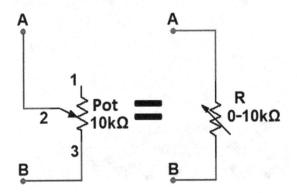

Figure 4-17. *Second method to make a variable resistor*

Rheostat

Rheostat (Figure 4-18) is a variable resistor, which is used to control the flow of electric current by manually increasing or decreasing the resistance. Rheostats can handle currents in the range of Amps.

Figure 4-18. *Sample rheostat*

The structure of a rheostat is shown in Figure 4-19. The three terminals of the rheostat are denoted as A, B, and C. Either A and B terminals or B and C terminals are used. In Figure 4-19, A and C are fixed and are connected toward the track which is known as the resistive element. Terminal B is connected to the slider (wiper). As the wiper moves, the length of the wire between input terminal (terminal A in Figure 4-19) and wiper changes. Therefore, the position of the wiper controls the resistance between A and B in Figure 4-19. Resistance between terminal A and C is constant since the length of wire between A and C is constant.

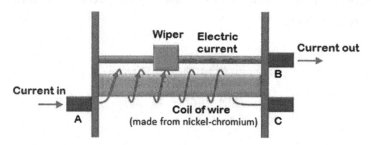

Figure 4-19. *Structure of a rheostat*

When wiper in Figure 4-19 moves toward right, number of turns between terminal A and wiper increases. This increases the length of wire between terminal A and wiper as well. Therefore, resistance between A and B increases when wiper moves toward right. The resistance between terminals A and B decreases when wiper moves toward left (Why?).

Commonly used symbols of rheostat are shown in Figure 4-20.

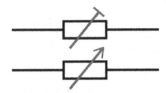

Figure 4-20. *Symbol of rheostat*

Light Dependent Resistor (LDR)

Light dependent resistors (LDRs) or photo resistors (Figure 4-21) are electronic components that are often used in electronic circuit designs where it is necessary to detect the presence or the level of light (for instance, photometer; Figure 4-22). Resistance of LDR is a function of the light that reaches to it.

Figure 4-21. *Sample LDR*

Figure 4-22. *Light meters use LDRs to measure the environment light intensity*

Commonly used symbols of LDR are shown in Figure 4-23.

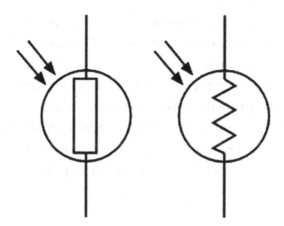

Figure 4-23. *LDR symbols*

Thermistor

A thermistor (Figure 4-24) is a resistor whose resistance is dependent on temperature. The term is a combination of "thermal" and "resistor." It is made of metallic oxides, pressed into a bead, disk, or cylindrical shape and then encapsulated with an impermeable material such as epoxy or glass.

Figure 4-24. NTC type thermistor

There are two types of thermistors: negative temperature coefficient (NTC) and positive temperature coefficient (PTC). With an NTC thermistor, when the temperature increases, resistance decreases. Conversely, when temperature decreases, resistance increases (Figure 4-25). This type of thermistor is used the most.

A PTC thermistor works a little differently. When temperature increases, the resistance increases, and when temperature decreases, resistance decreases (Figure 4-26). This type of thermistor is generally used as a fuse.

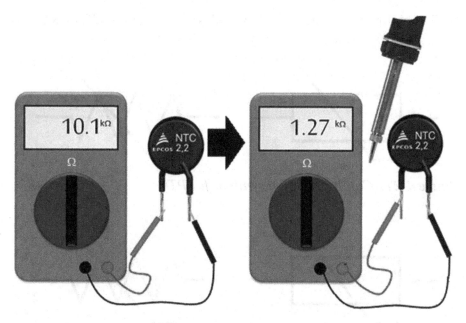

Figure 4-25. *Behavior of NTC type thermistors*

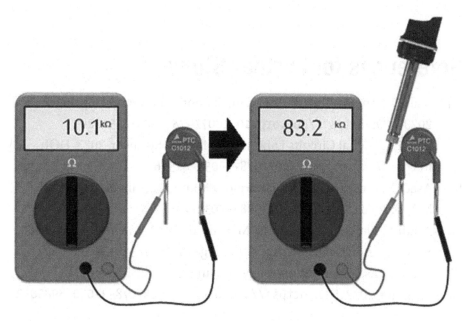

Figure 4-26. *Behavior of PTC type thermistors*

67

Commonly used symbols for PTC and NTC are shown in Figures 4-27 and 4-28, respectively.

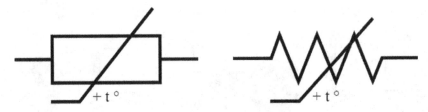

Figure 4-27. *Commonly used symbols for PTC*

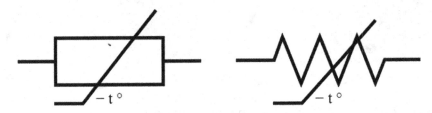

Figure 4-28. *Commonly used symbols for NTC*

References for Further Study

[1]   Asadi F., Analog Electronic Circuits Laboratory Manual, Springer, 2023. DOI: https://doi.org/10.1007/978-3-031-25122-1

[2]   Asadi F., Digital Circuits Laboratory Manual, Springer, 2023. DOI: https://doi.org/10.1007/978-3-031-41516-6

[3]   Asadi F., Electric Circuits Laboratory Manual, Springer, 2023. DOI: https://doi.org/10.1007/978-3-031-24552-7

[4]   Asadi F., Eguchi K., Electronic Measurement: A Practical Approach, Springer, 2021. DOI: https://doi.org/10.1007/978-3-031-02021-6

[5]   Asadi F., Essential Circuit Analysis using NI Multisim™ and MATLAB®, Springer, 2022. DOI: https://doi.org/10.1007/978-3-030-89850-2

[6]   Asadi F., Essential Circuit Analysis Using Proteus®, Springer, 2022. DOI: https://doi.org/10.1007/978-981-19-4353-9

[7]   Asadi F., Essential Circuit Analysis using LTspice®, Springer, 2022. DOI: https://doi.org/10.1007/978-3-031-09853-6

[8]   Asadi F., Electric and Electronic Circuit Simulation using TINA-TI®, River Publishers, 2022. DOI: https://doi.org/10.13052/rp-9788770226851

[9]   Asadi F., Electric Circuit Analysis with EasyEDA, Springer, 2022. DOI: https://doi.org/10.1007/978-3-031-00292-2

[10]   Asadi F., Power Electronics Circuit Analysis with PSIM®, De Gruyter, 2021. DOI: https://doi.org/10.1515/9783110740653

[11]   Asadi F., Simulation of Power Electronics Circuits with MATLAB®/Simulink®: Design, Analyze, and Prototype Power Electronics, Apress, 2022. DOI: https://doi.org/10.1007/978-1-4842-8220-5

[12]   Asadi F., Eguchi K., Simulation of Power Electronics Converters Using PLECS®, Academic Press, 2019. DOI: https://doi.org/10.1016/C2018-0-02253-7

CHAPTER 5

Diodes and Light-Emitting Diodes (LEDs)

A diode (Figure 5-1) is a semiconductor device that essentially acts as a one-way switch for current. It allows current to flow easily in one direction but severely restricts current from flowing in the opposite direction. Diode is one of the important components used in electronic circuits. This chapter studies the different types of diodes.

© Farzin Asadi 2024
F. Asadi, *ABCs of Electronics*, Maker Innovations Series,
https://doi.org/10.1007/979-8-8688-0134-1_5

Figure 5-1. *Different types of diodes*

Diode

The internal structure of a diode is shown in Figure 5-2. P-type materials are intrinsic crystals of silicon or germanium subjected to controlled impurification with chemical elements from the third column of the periodic table (e.g., boron or aluminum). N-type materials are intrinsic crystals of silicon or germanium subjected to controlled impurification with chemical elements from the fifth column of the periodic table (e.g., phosphorus, arsenic, antimony, bismuth).

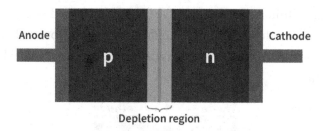

Figure 5-2. Structure of diode

The structure shown in Figure 5-3 permits current flow from anode to cathode. However, it blocks the current that wants to flow from cathode to anode. The reason of this phenomenon is beyond the scope of this book.

Diodes have two terminals: anode and cathode. The symbol of a diode is shown in Figure 5-3. The cathode terminal usually has a colored strip behind it (Figure 5-4).

Figure 5-3. Symbol of diode

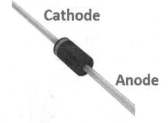

Figure 5-4. Cathode and anode terminals of a diode

Diodes are similar to one-way valve (Figure 5-5). In diodes, current flows only from anode to cathode. The diode is called "forward biased" when it conducts current. The diode is called "reverse biased" when it blocks current.

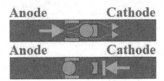

Figure 5-5. *The diode one-way valve analogy*

For instance, the lamp in Figure 5-6 turns on but the lamp in Figure 5-7 remains off. The diode in Figure 5-6 is forward biased while the diode in Figure 5-7 is reverse biased.

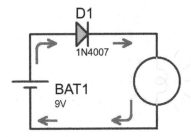

Figure 5-6. *Forward biased diode*

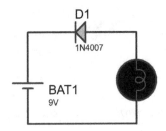

Figure 5-7. *Reverse biased diode*

A voltage drop is generated across a diode when it is forward biased. Generated voltage drop is almost independent of the current that passes through the diode. Typical value of generated voltage drop is around 0.6 V–0.7 V. A special type of diodes called "Schottky diodes" has a smaller voltage drop.

Rectification with Diodes

Rectification is one of the important applications of diodes. Rectification is the process of making a DC voltage from an AC voltage. Most of the adaptors (Figure 5-8) use the circuit shown in Figure 5-9 to generate a DC voltage from the main.

Figure 5-8. *A simple adaptor*

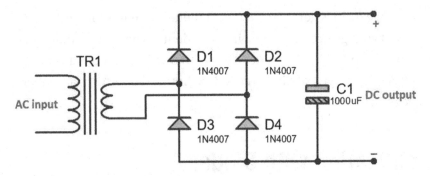

Figure 5-9. Internal circuit of a typical adaptor

Protection Against Polarity Reversal

Let's study another application of diodes. Polarity matters in sensitive electronic circuits. Some circuits can be easily destroyed by applying a reverse voltage. In this section, we will look at how to protect a circuit against reverse voltages by using diodes.

Consider a sensitive consumer which + and – terminals of input voltage must be connected to A and B, respectively (Figure 5-10). You can protect these devices by adding a diode in series (Figure 5-11).

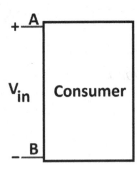

Figure 5-10. Sensitive consumer

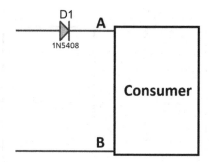

Figure 5-11. *A diode is used to protect the consumer against reverse polarity*

Let's see how series diode shown in Figure 5-11 protects the circuit. Assume that input voltage is connected similar to Figure 5-12. The diode is forward biased in this case and permits the current to pass through it. Therefore, the device is energized.

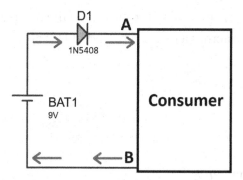

Figure 5-12. *The diode D1 is forward biased*

Now assume that reverse voltage is applied (Figure 5-13). The diode is reverse biased in this case and blocks the current flow. Therefore, the device is protected against reverse voltages.

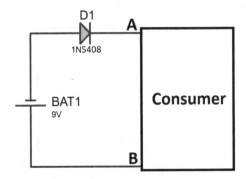

Figure 5-13. *The diode D1 is reverse biased*

Light-Emitting Diode (LED)

A light-emitting diode (LED; Figure 5-14) is a special diode that emits light when an electric current flows through it. LEDs allow the current to flow in the forward direction and blocks the current in the reverse direction. The typical voltage drop across a forward biased LED is around 1.5 V–2 V.

Figure 5-14. *A typical LED*

LEDs are commonly used as an indicator (Figure 5-15), source of light (Figure 5-16), or pixels of a display (Figure 5-17).

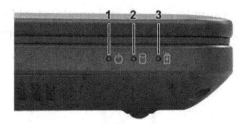

Figure 5-15. *LEDs are used as indicator*

Figure 5-16. *LEDs are used as light source in LED lamps*

Figure 5-17. *Dot-matrix display*

LEDs have two terminals: cathode and anode. The LED permits flow of current from anode to cathode only. The symbol of LED is shown in Figure 5-18.

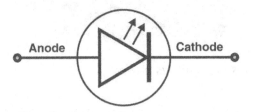

Figure 5-18. *LED symbol*

The following points help you to determine the anode and cathode of an LED easily:

a) LEDs have one lead that is longer that the other (Figure 5-19). This longer lead is the anode, and the shorter one is the cathode. Note that we assumed that the leads have not been clipped.

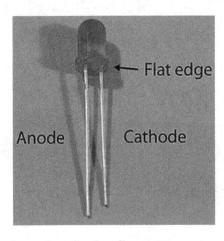

Figure 5-19. *Anode and cathode of an LED*

b) There is a small flat notch on the side of the
LED. The lead that is closer to the notch is always
the cathode (Figure 5-19).

Seven Segment Displays

Seven segment is a device to display decimal numerals. Seven segments
are composed of seven (or sometimes eight) LEDs. A typical seven
segment is shown in Figure 5-20. In Figure 5-20 a, b, c, d, e, f, and g, LEDs
are used to display decimal numbers, and the DP LED displays decimal
point. Figure 5-21 shows how different digits are displayed on a seven
segment display.

Figure 5-20. *Seven segment display*

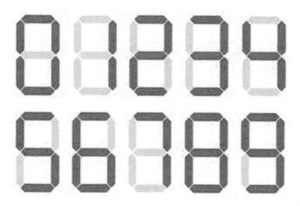

Figure 5-21. *Displaying numbers on seven segment displays*

Seven segment displays are divided into two groups: common cathode displays and common anode displays. The internal structure of common anode and common cathode displays is shown in Figure 5-22.

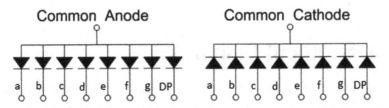

Figure 5-22. *Structure of common anode and common cathode seven segment displays*

Infrared Diodes

Remote controls (Figure 5-23) have a special type of LED which is placed into the pointing end of the handset. The LED in remote controls doesn't generate any visible light; it generates infrared light which is invisible with the naked eye.

Figure 5-23. *Most of remote controls use an infrared LED to send the commands*

When a button is pressed, the circuit inside the handset forces the LED to generate infrared light pulses. The pulses form a pattern unique to the pressed button. The receiver in the device recognizes the pattern and causes the device to respond accordingly.

Turning On the LED

Let's do a simple experiment with LEDs. The LED in Figure 5-24 turns on since it is forward biased. However, the LED in Figure 5-25 remains off since it is reverse biased. The resistor R1 in Figure 5-24 limits the current through the LED. Lower values of R1 (for instance, 470 Ω or 330 Ω) make the LED brighter.

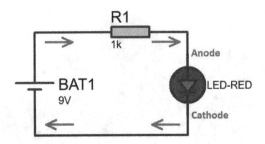

Figure 5-24. *Forward biased LED*

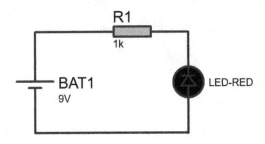

Figure 5-25. *Reversed biased LED*

Figures 5-26, 5-27, 5-28, and 5-29 show how to make the circuit shown in Figure 5-24 on a breadboard.

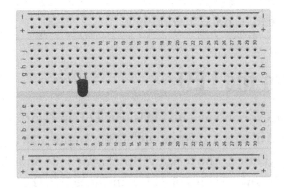

Figure 5-26. *Add an LED to the breadboard*

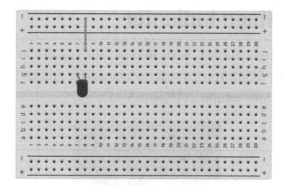

Figure 5-27. *Cathode of the LED is connected to the negative rail of the breadboard*

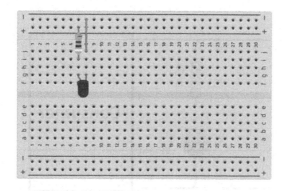

Figure 5-28. *A resistor is added to the breadboard*

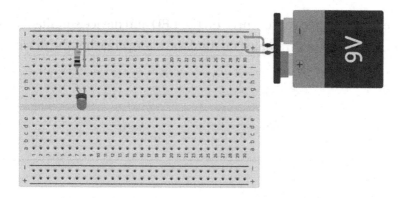

Figure 5-29. *Connect a battery to the supply rails of the breadboard*

85

LED as Voltage Indicator

Most of the electronic devices have an indicator, which shows the device is energized (Figure 5-30). You can connect a resistor and an LED in parallel to the device's supply terminals (Figure 5-31).

***Figure 5-30.** On LED shows the presence of input voltage*

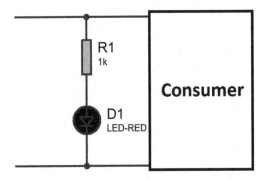

***Figure 5-31.** R1 and D1 make a simple voltage indicator*

The input voltage source turns on the LED and device simultaneously (Figure 5-32). The LED remains on until the energy reaches the device.

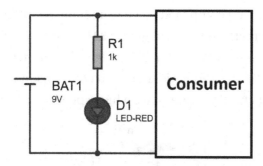

Figure 5-32. *The LED turns on when input voltage is given*

You can add the diode D2 to protect the consumer against polarity reversal as well (Figure 5-33).

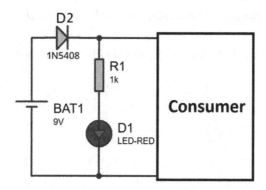

Figure 5-33. *Diode D2 protects the consumer against input reverse polarity*

Zener and Schottky Diodes

A Zener diode is a special type of diode designed to reliably allow current to flow "backward" (i.e., from cathode to anode) when a certain set reverse voltage, known as the Zener voltage, is reached. Zener diodes are used for voltage regulation purposes.

Normal diodes are composed of a PN junction. Schottky diodes have a semiconductor metal junction (Figure 5-34). A metal-semiconductor junction has metal in contact with the semiconductor material. Forward voltage drop of Schottky diodes is smaller in comparison with normal PN junction diodes. Schottky diodes have a high speed switching as well.

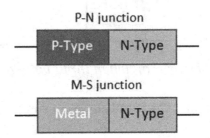

Figure 5-34. *Structure of normal and Schottky diodes*

The symbols for Zener and Schottky diodes are shown in Figure 5-35.

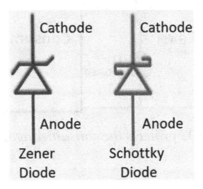

Figure 5-35. *Symbols of Zener and Schottky diodes*

References for Further Study

[1]   Asadi F., Analog Electronic Circuits Laboratory Manual, Springer, 2023. DOI: https://doi.org/10.1007/978-3-031-25122-1

[2]   Asadi F., Digital Circuits Laboratory Manual, Springer, 2023. DOI: https://doi.org/10.1007/978-3-031-41516-6

[3]   Asadi F., Electric Circuits Laboratory Manual, Springer, 2023. DOI: https://doi.org/10.1007/978-3-031-24552-7

[4]   Asadi F., Eguchi K., Electronic Measurement: A Practical Approach, Springer, 2021. DOI: https://doi.org/10.1007/978-3-031-02021-6

[5]   Asadi F., Essential Circuit Analysis using NI Multisim™ and MATLAB®, Springer, 2022. DOI: https://doi.org/10.1007/978-3-030-89850-2

[6]   Asadi F., Essential Circuit Analysis Using Proteus®, Springer, 2022. DOI: https://doi.org/10.1007/978-981-19-4353-9

[7]   Asadi F., Essential Circuit Analysis using LTspice®, Springer, 2022. DOI: https://doi.org/10.1007/978-3-031-09853-6

[8]   Asadi F., Electric and Electronic Circuit Simulation using TINA-TI®, River Publishers, 2022. DOI: https://doi.org/10.13052/rp-9788770226851

[9]   Asadi F., Electric Circuit Analysis with EasyEDA, Springer, 2022. DOI: https://doi.org/10.1007/978-3-031-00292-2

[10] Asadi F., Power Electronics Circuit Analysis with PSIM®, De Gruyter, 2021. DOI: https://doi.org/10.1515/9783110740653

[11] Asadi F., Simulation of Power Electronics Circuits with MATLAB®/Simulink®: Design, Analyze, and Prototype Power Electronics, Apress, 2022. DOI: https://doi.org/10.1007/978-1-4842-8220-5

[12] Asadi F., Eguchi K., Simulation of Power Electronics Converters Using PLECS®, Academic Press, 2019. DOI: https://doi.org/10.1016/C2018-0-02253-7

CHAPTER 6

Breadboard

A breadboard (Figure 6-1) is used for building temporary circuits. It is useful to designers because it allows components to be removed and replaced easily. It is useful to the person who wants to build a circuit to demonstrate its action and then to reuse the components in another circuit.

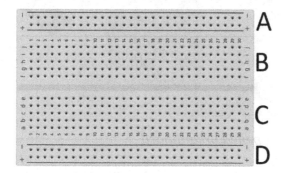

Figure 6-1. *A typical breadboard*

Breadboard holes are connected to each other according to the pattern shown in Figure 6-2. The long horizontal rails with + and – labels are usually connected to the energy source (i.e., a battery). The inside of a breadboard is shown in Figure 6-3.

© Farzin Asadi 2024
F. Asadi, *ABCs of Electronics*, Maker Innovations Series,
https://doi.org/10.1007/979-8-8688-0134-1_6

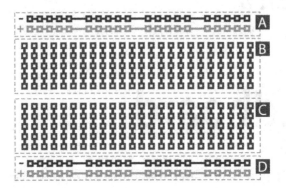

Figure 6-2. *Connections of breadboard*

Figure 6-3. *An opened breadboard*

This chapter shows how to use a breadboard in order to prototype a circuit.

Sample Circuit

Let's study an example. Assume that we want to make the circuit shown in Figure 6-4 on a breadboard.

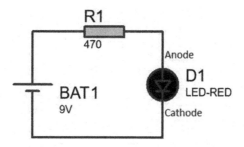

Figure 6-4. *A simple circuit*

Let's get started. Add a 470 Ω resistor to the breadboard (Figure 6-5). The upper terminal of the 470 Ω resistor is connected to the + rail.

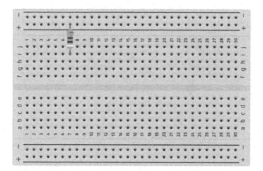

Figure 6-5. *A resistor is added to the breadboard*

Add an LED to the breadboard (Figure 6-6). The anode of the LED is connected to the 470 Ω resistor.

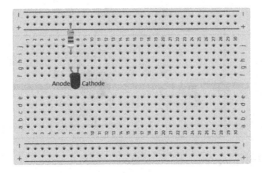

Figure 6-6. *An LED is added to the breadboard*

Use a piece of wire to connect the LED to the negative rail (Figure 6-7).

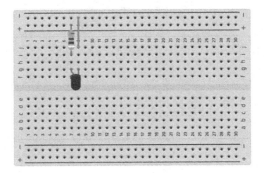

Figure 6-7. *Cathode of the LED is connected to the negative rail of the breadboard*

Connect a battery to the + and – rails (Figure 6-8). The LED turns on after connecting the power.

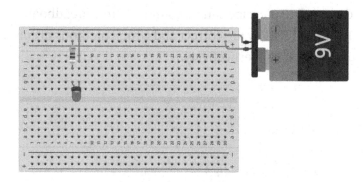

Figure 6-8. *Battery is connected to the breadboard*

Placing the ICs on the Breadboard

Different ICs have different packages. Some of the most famous packages are dual-in-line package (DIP), surface-mount device (SMD), small-outline IC (SOIC), small-outline package (SOP), quad-flat package (QFP), quad-flat no-leads (QFN), small-outline transistor (SOT), and ball-grid array (BGA). These packages are shown in Figure 6-9.

Figure 6-9. *Different IC packages*

95

Only ICs with DIP package can be connected to a breadboard.
Figures 6-10 and 6-11 show the correct and wrong methods of connecting
a DIP IC to a breadboard, respectively.

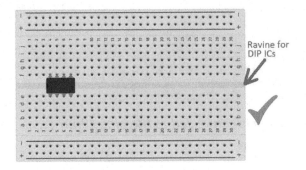

Figure 6-10. *Correct method of connecting a DIP IC to a breadboard*

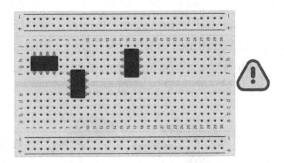

Figure 6-11. *Wrong methods of connecting a DIP IC to a breadboard*

References for Further Study

[1]   Asadi F., Analog Electronic Circuits Laboratory Manual, Springer,
       2023. DOI: https://doi.org/10.1007/978-3-031-25122-1

[2]   Asadi F., Digital Circuits Laboratory Manual, Springer, 2023. DOI:
       https://doi.org/10.1007/978-3-031-41516-6

[3]   Asadi F., Electric Circuits Laboratory Manual, Springer, 2023. DOI: https://doi.org/10.1007/978-3-031-24552-7

[4]   Asadi F., Eguchi K., Electronic Measurement: A Practical Approach, Springer, 2021. DOI: https://doi.org/10.1007/978-3-031-02021-6

[5]   Asadi F., Essential Circuit Analysis using NI Multisim™ and MATLAB®, Springer, 2022. DOI: https://doi.org/10.1007/978-3-030-89850-2

[6]   Asadi F., Essential Circuit Analysis Using Proteus®, Springer, 2022. DOI: https://doi.org/10.1007/978-981-19-4353-9

[7]   Asadi F., Essential Circuit Analysis using LTspice®, Springer, 2022. DOI: https://doi.org/10.1007/978-3-031-09853-6

[8]   Asadi F., Electric and Electronic Circuit Simulation using TINA-TI®, River Publishers, 2022. DOI: https://doi.org/10.13052/rp-9788770226851

[9]   Asadi F., Electric Circuit Analysis with EasyEDA, Springer, 2022. DOI: https://doi.org/10.1007/978-3-031-00292-2

[10]   Asadi F., Power Electronics Circuit Analysis with PSIM®, De Gruyter, 2021. DOI: https://doi.org/10.1515/9783110740653

[11]   Asadi F., Simulation of Power Electronics Circuits with MATLAB®/ Simulink®: Design, Analyze, and Prototype Power Electronics, Apress, 2022. DOI: https://doi.org/10.1007/978-1-4842-8220-5

[12]   Asadi F., Eguchi K., Simulation of Power Electronics Converters Using PLECS®, Academic Press, 2019. DOI: https://doi.org/10.1016/C2018-0-02253-7

CHAPTER 7

Bipolar Junction Transistors (BJTs)

William Shockley, John Bardeen, and Walter Brattain invented the transistor in 1947. The term "transistor" is derived from the words "transfer" and "resistor." These words describe the operation of a BJT which is the transfer of an input signal from a low resistance circuit to a high resistance circuit.

Transistors are one of the important components that are used in electronic circuits. Transistors are used for amplification or switching purposes. In simple words, amplification is the process of increasing the magnitude of a signal. The device which does the amplification is called an amplifier. Amplification process is shown in Figure 7-1.

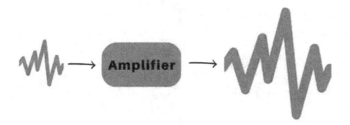

Figure 7-1. *Amplification process*

Switching is the process of connecting or interrupting a current. Switching process is shown in Figure 7-2.

© Farzin Asadi 2024
F. Asadi, *ABCs of Electronics*, Maker Innovations Series,
https://doi.org/10.1007/979-8-8688-0134-1_7

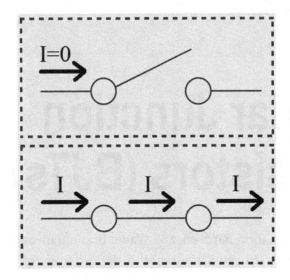

Figure 7-2. *Open and closed switches*

This chapter focuses on bipolar junction transistors (BJTs). A bipolar junction transistor is a three terminal semiconductor device that consists of two p-n junctions (Figure 7-3).

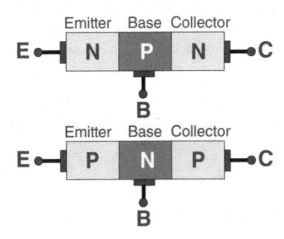

Figure 7-3. *Internal structure of NPN and PNP transistors*

P-type materials are intrinsic crystals of silicon or germanium subjected to controlled impurification with chemical elements from the third column of the periodic table (e.g., boron or aluminum).

N-type materials are intrinsic crystals of silicon or germanium subjected to controlled impurification with chemical elements from the fifth column of the periodic table (e.g., phosphorus, arsenic, antimony, bismuth).

This chapter doesn't study the internal structure and working principles of BJT transistors since these subjects are not important for makers. Some BJTs are shown in Figures 7-4, 7-5, 7-6, and 7-7. Most of the circuits in this chapter are made with BC237 transistor (Figure 7-4).

Figure 7-4. *A BJT transistor with TO-92 package*

Figure 7-5. *A BJT transistor with TO-220 package*

Figure 7-6. *A BJT transistor with TO-3 package*

Figure 7-7. *A BJT transistor with SMD package*

NPN and PNP Transistors

Internal structures of NPN and PNP transistors are shown in Figure 7-3. Some circuits require NPN transistors, while the others use PNP transistors. Therefore, both types are useful. However, most of the circuits use NPN transistors. The symbols for NPN and PNP transistors are shown in Figures 7-8 and 7-9, respectively.

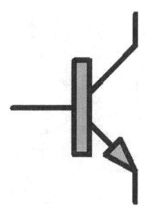

Figure 7-8. *Symbol of NPN transistor*

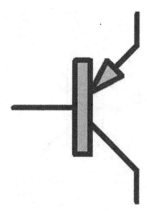

Figure 7-9. *Symbol of PNP transistor*

BJT transistors have three terminals: base (B), collector (C), and emitter (E). Figures 7-10 and 7-11 show the base, collector, and emitter terminals of NPN and PNP transistors, respectively. Usually metal case of the power transistors (Figures 7-5 and 7-6) is connected to the collector terminal.

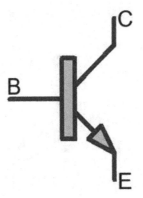

Figure 7-10. *Base, collector, and emitter terminals of an NPN transistor*

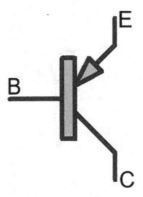

Figure 7-11. *Base, collector, and emitter terminals of a PNP transistor*

Directions of current flow for NPN and PNP transistors are shown in Figures 7-12 and 7-13, respectively. Emitter current equals the summation of base and collector currents for both cases ($I_E = I_B + I_C$).

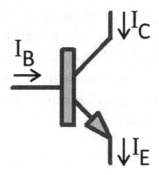

Figure 7-12. *Base, collector, and emitter currents in NPN transistor*
$(I_B + I_C = I_E)$

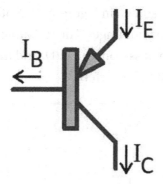

Figure 7-13. *Base, collector, and emitter currents in PNP transistor*
$(I_B + I_C = I_E)$

Datasheet and Pinout of a Transistor

Each transistor has a datasheet which contains useful information about it. You can see the pinout of a specific transistor by writing the transistor number followed by the word "datasheet" in Google. For instance, you can obtain the datasheet of BC237 by searching the "BC237 datasheet" in Google.

You can see the pinout of a specific transistor by writing the transistor number followed by the word "pinout" in Google Images. For instance, you can write "BC237 pinout" in Google Images to obtain the pinout of BC237. Reference [1] shows how pins of a transistor can be determined with the aid of a digital multimeter. You can use the digital multimeter to see whether the transistor is faulty.

Touch Switch

A touch switch is a type of switch that only has to be touched by an object to operate. In this section, we want to make a touch switch to turn on an LED. Consider the circuit shown in Figure 7-14. Nothing will happen if you touch points A and B with your finger. The resistance of your finger doesn't permit enough current to pass from the LED, and the LED remains off. So, we need a circuit to amplify the current.

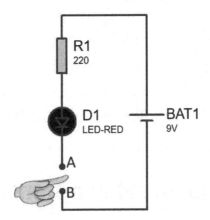

Figure 7-14. *You cannot turn on the LED by touching the A and B points*

A touch switch circuit is shown in Figure 7-15. The two transistors shown in Figure 7-15 amplify the current to the level which is able to turn on the LED. Pinout of the used transistor is shown in Figure 7-16.

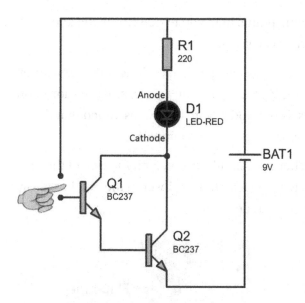

Figure 7-15. *The LED is turned on by touching the A and B points*

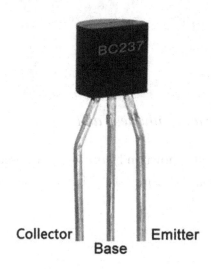

Figure 7-16. *Base, collector, and emitter terminals of BC 237 transistor*

107

The following points help you to determine the anode and cathode of an LED (Figure 7-17) easily:

a) LEDs have one lead that is longer than the other. This longer lead is the anode, and the shorter one is the cathode. Note that we assumed that the leads have not been clipped.

b) There is a small flat notch on the side of the LED. The lead that is closer to the notch is always the cathode.

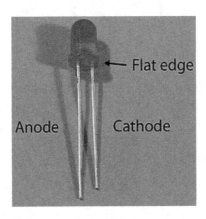

Figure 7-17. *Anode and cathode of an LED*

Let's make the circuit shown in Figure 7-15 on a breadboard. Put a BC237 on the breadboard (Figure 7-18). This transistor plays the role of Q1 in Figure 7-15.

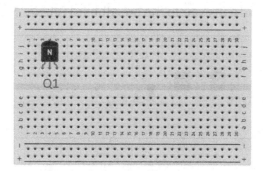

Figure 7-18. *Q1 is added to the breadboard*

Put another BC237 on the breadboard (Figure 7-19). This second transistor plays the role of Q2 in Figure 7-15.

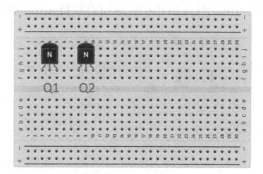

Figure 7-19. *Q2 is added to the breadboard*

Add an LED and a resistor to the breadboard (Figure 7-20).

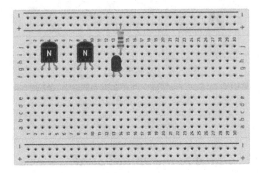

Figure 7-20. *The LED and 220 Ω resistor are added to the breadboard*

Connect the emitter of Q1 to the base of Q2 (Figure 7-21).

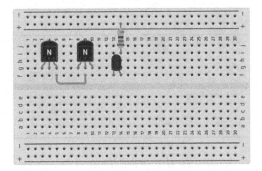

Figure 7-21. *Emitter of Q1 is connected to base of Q2*

Connect the collector of Q1 to the collector of Q2 (Figure 7-22).

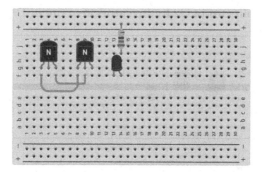

Figure 7-22. *Collector of Q1 is connected to collector of Q2*

Connect the emitter of Q2 to the negative rail of the breadboard (Figure 7-23).

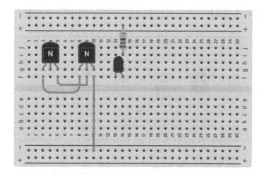

Figure 7-23. *Emitter of Q2 is connected to negative rail of the breadboard*

Connect the collector of Q2 to the cathode of the LED (Figure 7-24).

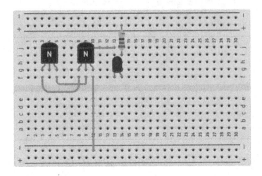

Figure 7-24. *Collector of Q2 is connected to cathode of the LED*

Connect a wire to base of Q1 and another one to the positive rail of the breadboard (Figure 7-25).

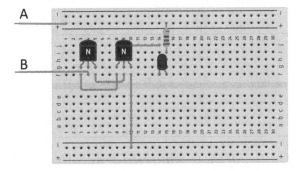

Figure 7-25. *Two wires are connected to base of Q1 and positive rail of the breadboard*

Connect a battery to the positive and negative rail of the breadboard (Figure 7-26).

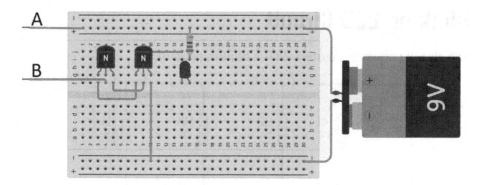

Figure 7-26. *A battery is connected to the breadboard*

Touch the wires (Figure 7-27). When you touch the wires, the LED turns on.

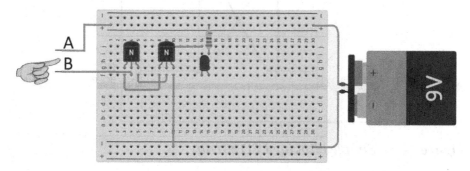

Figure 7-27. *The LED turns on when the tip of the wires is touched*

Blinking LED Circuit

The circuit shown in Figure 7-28 is a blinking circuit.

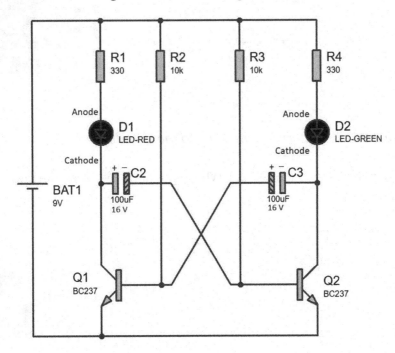

Figure 7-28. *Simple blinking LED circuit*

Make the circuit on a breadboard, and ensure that it works properly. + and – terminals of electrolytic capacitors are shown in Figure 7-29.

Figure 7-29. *Negative terminal has a "-" marking and/or a colored strip along the can*

Audio Amplifier

A simple audio amplifier circuit is shown in Figure 7-30. Make the circuit on the breadboard. Connect the wires A and B to the right audio and ground terminals of an audio jack, respectively (Figure 7-31). Connect the audio jack to an old computer or a cell phone, and play a music to test the circuit.

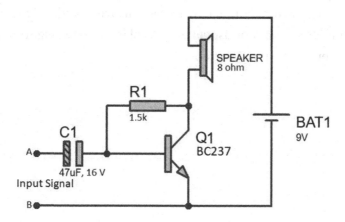

Figure 7-30. *Simple audio amplifier circuit*

Ground

Right Audio

Left Audio

Figure 7-31. *Audio jack*

Loudspeaker

Section 7.6 used a loudspeaker to generate sound. Loudspeaker is an electroacoustic transducer that converts an electrical audio signal into a corresponding sound. Loudspeaker symbol is shown in Figure 7-32. A loudspeaker is shown in Figure 7-33.

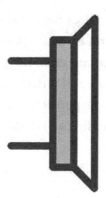

Figure 7-32. *Loudspeaker symbol*

Figure 7-33. *Speaker*

Structure of a loudspeaker is shown in Figure 7-34. Let's see how a loudspeaker works. An amplifier feeds a signal to two terminals on the back of a speaker. These terminals pass the current into a cylindrical coil of wire, which is suspended in the circular gap between the poles of a

117

permanent magnet. This coil moves back and forth inside the magnetic field as the current passing through it alternates in direction with the signal applied, per Faraday's law. The center of the speaker cone is attached to one end, which gets driven back and forth by the moving coil. This cone is held at its edges by an airtight suspension or surround. As the cone moves, it pushes and pulls the surrounding air; by doing so, it creates pressure waves in the air, called sound.

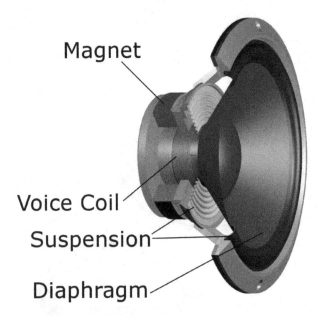

Figure 7-34. *Standard speaker structure*

Heat Sink

A heat sink is a passive heat exchanger that transfers the heat generated by an electronic device to air, where it is dissipated away from the device, thereby allowing regulation of the device's temperature. A sample heat sink is shown in Figure 7-35.

Figure 7-35. *A typical heat sink*

Transistors dissipate a part of energy in the form of heat. The generated heat must be removed from the transistor; otherwise, device temperature increases, and this may destroy the device. In Figure 7-36, transistors are attached to heat sinks in order to decrease the transistor temperature (The presence of heat sink facilitates heat transfer from the transistor to the ambient air.). Some heat sinks use a fan to further reduce the device temperature (Figure 7-37).

Figure 7-36. *Transistors are mounted to the heat sink in order to decrease the device temperature*

Figure 7-37. *Fan-cooled heat sink*

References for Further Study

[1] Asadi F., Analog Electronic Circuits Laboratory Manual, Springer, 2023. DOI: https://doi.org/10.1007/978-3-031-25122-1

[2] Asadi F., Digital Circuits Laboratory Manual, Springer, 2023. DOI: https://doi.org/10.1007/978-3-031-41516-6

[3] Asadi F., Electric Circuits Laboratory Manual, Springer, 2023. DOI: https://doi.org/10.1007/978-3-031-24552-7

[4] Asadi F., Eguchi K., Electronic Measurement: A Practical Approach, Springer, 2021. DOI: https://doi.org/10.1007/978-3-031-02021-6

[5] Asadi F., Essential Circuit Analysis using NI Multisim™ and MATLAB®, Springer, 2022. DOI: https://doi.org/10.1007/978-3-030-89850-2

[6] Asadi F., Essential Circuit Analysis Using Proteus®, Springer, 2022. DOI: https://doi.org/10.1007/978-981-19-4353-9

[7] Asadi F., Essential Circuit Analysis using LTspice®, Springer, 2022. DOI: https://doi.org/10.1007/978-3-031-09853-6

[8] Asadi F., Electric and Electronic Circuit Simulation using TINA-TI®, River Publishers, 2022. DOI: https://doi.org/10.13052/rp-9788770226851

[9]   Asadi F., Electric Circuit Analysis with EasyEDA, Springer, 2022. DOI: https://doi.org/10.1007/978-3-031-00292-2

[10] Asadi F., Power Electronics Circuit Analysis with PSIM®, De Gruyter, 2021. DOI: https://doi.org/10.1515/9783110740653

[11] Asadi F., Simulation of Power Electronics Circuits with MATLAB®/ Simulink®: Design, Analyze, and Prototype Power Electronics, Apress, 2022. DOI: https://doi.org/10.1007/978-1-4842-8220-5

[12] Asadi F., Eguchi K., Simulation of Power Electronics Converters Using PLECS®, Academic Press, 2019. DOI: https://doi.org/10.1016/ C2018-0-02253-7

CHAPTER 8

Metal-Oxide Semiconductor Field-Effect Transistor (MOSFET)

BJTs were studied in the previous chapter. Metal-oxide semiconductor field-effect transistor (MOSFET) (Figures 8-1 and 8-2) is another important type of transistor that is used in electronic circuits. MOSFETs are electronic devices used to switch or amplify voltages in circuits. It is a voltage controlled device and is constructed by three terminals. The terminals of MOSFET are named as follows: gate, drain, and source. This chapter studies the MOSFETs.

© Farzin Asadi 2024
F. Asadi, *ABCs of Electronics*, Maker Innovations Series,
https://doi.org/10.1007/979-8-8688-0134-1_8

Figure 8-1. *A MOSFET transistor with TO-220 package*

Figure 8-2. *A MOSFET transistor with SMD package*

MOSFETs are of two classes: enhancement mode and depletion mode. Each class is available as N-channel or P-channel; hence, overall they tally up to four types of MOSFETs (Figure 8-3).

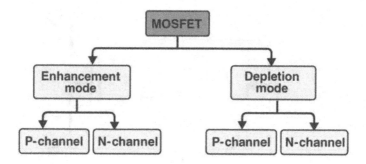

Figure 8-3. *Different types of MOSFETs*

The N-channel MOSFETs are abbreviated as NMOS and are symbolically represented as shown in Figure 8-4.

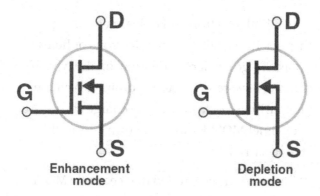

Figure 8-4. *Symbols of N-channel MOSFET*

Similarly, the P-channel MOSFETs are abbreviated as PMOS and are symbolically represented as shown in Figure 8-5.

125

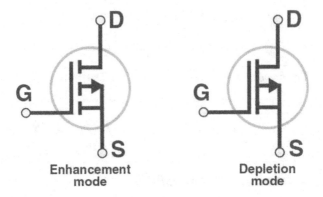

Figure 8-5. *Symbols of P-channel MOSFET*

Let's see some of the differences between BJT and MOSFET:

A) In BJT, both electron and holes act as charge carriers. In MOSFET, either electrons or holes act as charge carriers depending on the type of channel between source and drain. A P-channel MOSFET uses hole flow as the charge carrier. An N-channel MOSFET uses electron flow as the charge carrier.

B) BJT is a current-controlled device, while MOSFET is a voltage-controlled device.

C) BJT consumes more power in comparison with MOSFET.

D) Based on construction, BJTs are classified into two types: NPN and PNP. MOSFETs are classified into four types: P-channel enhancement MOSFET, N-channel enhancement MOSFET, P-channel depletion MOSFET, and N-channel depletion MOSFET.

E) MOSFETs are vulnerable to damage by
electrostatic charges due to the thin oxide layer.
BJTs are not.

MOSFET as Switch

MOSFETs are commonly used as switch. When gate-source voltage is
big enough (i.e., it is bigger than the threshold voltage of the device), the
drain-source acts as short circuit, and drain-source terminals play the role
of a closed switch.

When gate-source voltage is small enough (i.e., it is less than the
threshold voltage of the device), the drain-source acts as open circuit, and
drain-source terminals play the role of an open switch.

In other words, the gate-source voltage determines the status of the
switch. Let's use a simple experiment to understand this subject.

Make the circuit shown in Figure 8-6 on a breadboard. Pinout of
IRFZ41 is shown in Figure 8-7. You can obtain the pinout of any device by
searching the Google Images. For instance, you can search for "IRFZ41
pinout" in Google Images to see the pinout of IRFZ41 N-channel MOSFET.

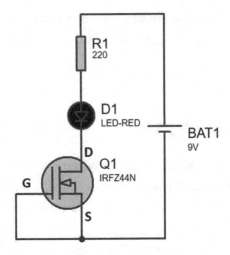

Figure 8-6. *LED remains off ($V_{GS} = 0$ V)*

Figure 8-7. *Pinout of IRFZ 44N*

In Figure 8-6, the gate-source voltage is zero (gate and source are connected together; therefore, they have the same potential, and there is no difference between them, i.e., $V_{gate} - V_{source} = 0$), and the MOSFET plays the role of an open switch. The LED is off since no current passes through it.

Now connect the gate to positive terminal of the battery. In Figure 8-8, the gate-source voltage is 9 V. 9 V is big enough to force the IRFZ 41 to act as a closed switch. Therefore, in Figure 8-8, the LED turns on.

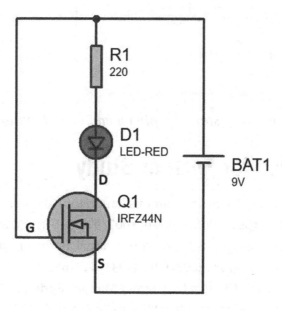

Figure 8-8. *LED turns on ($V_{GS} = 9$ V)*

Let's use the MOSFET to turn on/off a small DC motor. In Figure 8-9, the motor spins when the push button is pressed. The motor stops when the push button is released. The diode D1 protects the MOSFET against the transient (high) voltages that are generated by the motor.

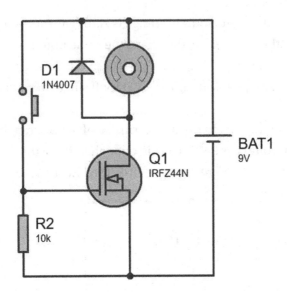

Figure 8-9. *The motor starts to spin when the push button is pressed*

References for Further Study

[1]   Asadi F., Analog Electronic Circuits Laboratory Manual, Springer, 2023. DOI: https://doi.org/10.1007/978-3-031-25122-1

[2]   Asadi F., Digital Circuits Laboratory Manual, Springer, 2023. DOI: https://doi.org/10.1007/978-3-031-41516-6

[3]   Asadi F., Electric Circuits Laboratory Manual, Springer, 2023. DOI: https://doi.org/10.1007/978-3-031-24552-7

[4]   Asadi F., Eguchi K., Electronic Measurement: A Practical Approach, Springer, 2021. DOI: https://doi.org/10.1007/978-3-031-02021-6

[5]   Asadi F., Essential Circuit Analysis using NI Multisim™ and MATLAB®, Springer, 2022. DOI: https://doi.org/10.1007/978-3-030-89850-2

[6]   Asadi F., Essential Circuit Analysis Using Proteus®, Springer, 2022. DOI: https://doi.org/10.1007/978-981-19-4353-9

[7]   Asadi F., Essential Circuit Analysis using LTspice®, Springer, 2022. DOI: https://doi.org/10.1007/978-3-031-09853-6

[8]   Asadi F., Electric and Electronic Circuit Simulation using TINA-TI°, River Publishers, 2022. DOI: https://doi.org/10.13052/rp-9788770226851

[9]   Asadi F., Electric Circuit Analysis with EasyEDA, Springer, 2022. DOI: https://doi.org/10.1007/978-3-031-00292-2

[10] Asadi F., Power Electronics Circuit Analysis with PSIM°, De Gruyter, 2021. DOI: https://doi.org/10.1515/9783110740653

[11] Asadi F., Simulation of Power Electronics Circuits with MATLAB°/Simulink°: Design, Analyze, and Prototype Power Electronics, Apress, 2022. DOI: https://doi.org/10.1007/978-1-4842-8220-5

[12] Asadi F., Eguchi K., Simulation of Power Electronics Converters Using PLECS°, Academic Press, 2019. DOI: https://doi.org/10.1016/C2018-0-02253-7

CHAPTER 9

Relays

Relay (Figure 9-1) is an electromechanical switch. You can use a relatively small current to control a large current. Relays are thousand and million times slower than electronic switches like BJT and MOSFETs.

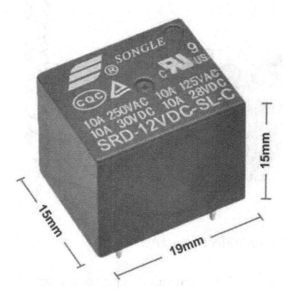

Figure 9-1. *A typical relay*

We need to learn what an electromagnet is in order to understand how relays work. An electromagnet is a type of magnet in which the magnetic field is produced by an electric current. Electromagnets usually consist of wire wound into a coil. A current through the wire creates a magnetic field which is concentrated in the hole in the center of the coil. The magnetic

© Farzin Asadi 2024
F. Asadi, *ABCs of Electronics*, Maker Innovations Series,
https://doi.org/10.1007/979-8-8688-0134-1_9

field disappears when the current is turned off. The wire turns are often wound around a magnetic core made from a ferromagnetic material such as iron; the magnetic core concentrates the magnetic flux and makes a more powerful magnet. You can make an electromagnet with a nail and few turns of wire (Figure 9-2). You can lift small paper clips with such an electromagnet.

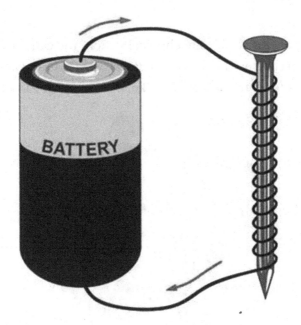

Figure 9-2. *A simple electromagnet*

Each relay has a coil. The current that passes through the coil makes an electromagnet. The electromagnet closes or opens the relay's contacts (Figure 9-3). Symbol of a relay is shown in Figure 9-4.

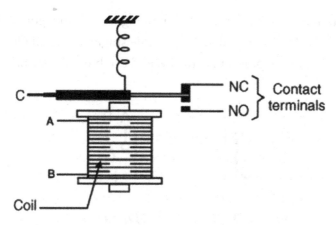

Figure 9-3. *Structure of a relay*

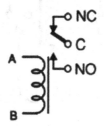

Figure 9-4. *Symbol of a relay (NC: normally close; NO: normally open)*

Let's see how the relay shown in Figure 9-3 works. The spring pulls the armature C upward, and it forces the C to hit the NC terminal when no energy is applied to the coil. When coil is energized, an electromagnet is formed and absorbs the armature C downward. When armature C goes down hits the terminal NO and a connection between C and NO is formed. When coil is not energized, the springer brings the armature C upward and it hits the NC again.

Important types of relays are shown in Figure 9-5. In Figure 9-5, SPST, SPDT, DPST, and DPDT stand for single pole single throw, single pole double throw, double pole single throw, and double pole double throw, respectively.

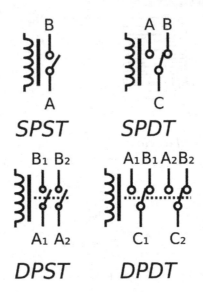

Figure 9-5. *Important types of relays*

Each relay works with a certain voltage. The required operating voltage for the coil and current allowed to pass through relay contacts is printed on the relay case. For instance, for the relay shown in Figure 9-6, the operating voltage for the coil is 12 V. The contacts of this relay can handle 250 VAC/10 A or 30 VDC/10 A load.

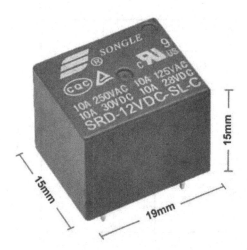

Figure 9-6. *Operating voltage and current are printed on the relay*

Transistor Relay Driver

The circuits shown in Figures 9-7 and 9-8 can be used to turn on/off a relay. The relay coil is energized when the push button in Figure 9-7 or 9-8 is pressed. When relay coil is energized, common terminal C is connected to NO and turns on the lamp.

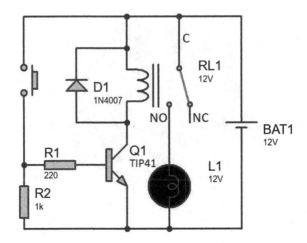

Figure 9-7. *Driving a relay with BJT transistor*

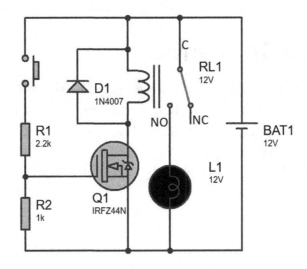

Figure 9-8. *Driving a relay with MOSFET transistor*

Make the circuits shown in Figures 9-7 and 9-8 on breadboard, and ensure that they work as expected. Pinout of TIP 41 and IRFZ 44N are shown in Figure 9-9. Use Google to obtain the pinout of your relay.

Figure 9-9. *Pinout of IRFZ 44N and TIP 41*

References for Further Study

[1] Asadi F., Analog Electronic Circuits Laboratory Manual, Springer, 2023. DOI: https://doi.org/10.1007/978-3-031-25122-1

[2] Asadi F., Digital Circuits Laboratory Manual, Springer, 2023. DOI: https://doi.org/10.1007/978-3-031-41516-6

[3] Asadi F., Electric Circuits Laboratory Manual, Springer, 2023. DOI: https://doi.org/10.1007/978-3-031-24552-7

[4] Asadi F., Eguchi K., Electronic Measurement: A Practical Approach, Springer, 2021. DOI: https://doi.org/10.1007/978-3-031-02021-6

[5] Asadi F., Essential Circuit Analysis using NI Multisim™ and MATLAB®, Springer, 2022. DOI: https://doi.org/10.1007/978-3-030-89850-2

[6] Asadi F., Essential Circuit Analysis Using Proteus®, Springer, 2022.
     DOI: https://doi.org/10.1007/978-981-19-4353-9

[7] Asadi F., Essential Circuit Analysis using LTspice®, Springer, 2022. DOI:
     https://doi.org/10.1007/978-3-031-09853-6

[8] Asadi F., Electric and Electronic Circuit Simulation using TINA-
     TI®, River Publishers, 2022. DOI: https://doi.org/10.13052/
     rp-9788770226851

[9] Asadi F., Electric Circuit Analysis with EasyEDA, Springer, 2022. DOI:
     https://doi.org/10.1007/978-3-031-00292-2

[10] Asadi F., Power Electronics Circuit Analysis with PSIM®, De Gruyter,
     2021. DOI: https://doi.org/10.1515/9783110740653

[11] Asadi F., Simulation of Power Electronics Circuits with MATLAB®/
     Simulink®: Design, Analyze, and Prototype Power Electronics, Apress,
     2022. DOI: https://doi.org/10.1007/978-1-4842-8220-5

[12] Asadi F., Eguchi K., Simulation of Power Electronics Converters Using
     PLECS®, Academic Press, 2019. DOI: https://doi.org/10.1016/
     C2018-0-02253-7

CHAPTER 10

Integrated Circuits (ICs)

An integrated circuit or monolithic integrated circuit (also referred to as an IC, a chip, or a microchip) is a set of electronic circuits on one small flat piece (or "chip") of semiconductor material, usually silicon.

Large numbers of miniaturized transistors and other electronic components are integrated together on the chip. This results in circuits that are orders of magnitude smaller, faster, and less expensive than those constructed of discrete components, allowing a large transistor count.

The IC's mass production capability, reliability, and building-block approach to integrated circuit design have ensured the rapid adoption of standardized ICs in place of designs using discrete transistors.

ICs are now used in virtually all electronic equipment and have revolutionized the world of electronics. Each IC is designed for a specific task. A circuit with six ICs is shown in Figure 10-1.

© Farzin Asadi 2024
F. Asadi, *ABCs of Electronics*, Maker Innovations Series,
https://doi.org/10.1007/979-8-8688-0134-1_10

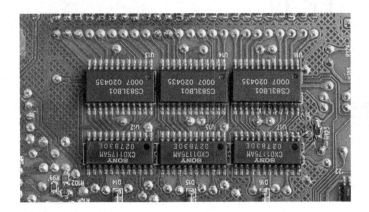

Figure 10-1. *Six ICs are used in this board*

IC Packages and Pin Numbering

Different ICs have different packages. Some of the most famous packages are dual-in-line package (DIP), surface-mount device (SMD), small-outline IC (SOIC), small-outline package (SOP), quad-flat package (QFP), quad-flat no-leads (QFN), small-outline transistor (SOT), and ball-grid array (BGA). These packages are shown in Figure 10-2.

Figure 10-2. *Different IC packages*

Most of IC vendors show the first pin of the IC with a small circle. Figures 10-3 and 10-4 show how IC pins are numbered.

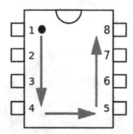

Figure 10-3. *Numbering of pins in DIP packages*

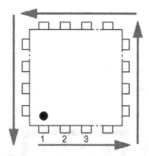

Figure 10-4. *Numbering of pins in QFP packages*

Each IC has its own datasheet, which contains useful information about that IC. You can use Google to obtain the datasheet. For instance, you can search for "LM741 datasheet" in Google to obtain the LM741 operational amplifier datasheet.

In the next sections, we will make some circuits with some of the commonly used ICs.

555 Timer IC

555 IC (Figure 10-5) is used in a variety of timer, delay, pulse generation, and oscillator applications. Pinout of this IC is shown in Figure 10-6.

Figure 10-5. *555 timer IC*

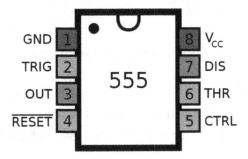

Figure 10-6. *Pinout of 555 timer IC*

Let's make a blinking LED circuit with this IC. Make the circuit shown in Figure 10-7 on a breadboard, and test it. Replace the C2 capacitor with a 10 µF capacitor, and see what happens.

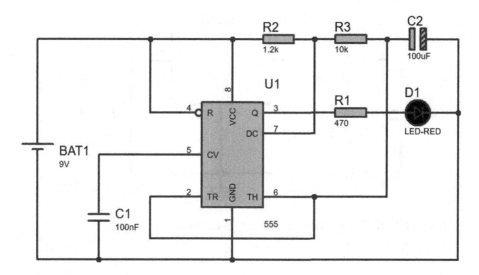

Figure 10-7. Blinking LED circuit with 555 IC

UM 66 IC

UM 66 (Figure 10-8) is a melody integrated circuit. UM 66 is used in calling bell, phone, toys and musical bell in doors, home security alarm systems, burglar alarms, etc.

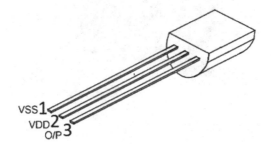

Figure 10-8. UM66 IC

Make the circuit shown in Figure 10-9. When you close the switch, a melody is played.

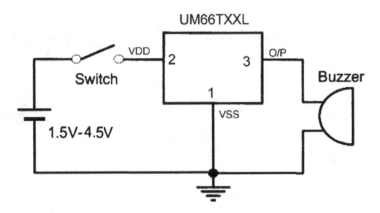

Figure 10-9. *UM 66 plays a melody when switch is closed*

LM 386 IC

LM 386 (Figure 10-10) is a low voltage audio power amplifier. Pinout of this IC is shown in Figure 10-11. You can make an amplifier with this IC and a few external components.

Figure 10-10. *LM386N IC*

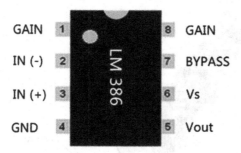

Figure 10-11. *Pinout of LM 386 IC*

Let's make an amplifier with this IC. Make the circuit shown in Figure 10-12 on a breadboard. Connect the point x and y to left audio and ground terminals of an audio jack, respectively (Figure 10-13). Connect the audio jack to an old computer or a cell phone, and play a music to test the circuit. The 10 kΩ potentiometer controls the loudness, that is, plays the role of volume.

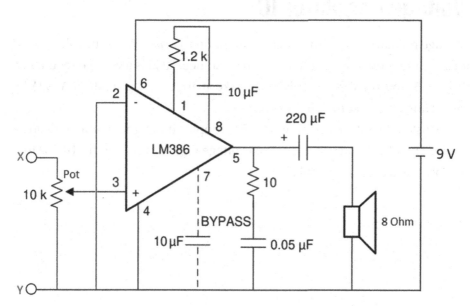

Figure 10-12. *An audio amplifier circuit with LM 386*

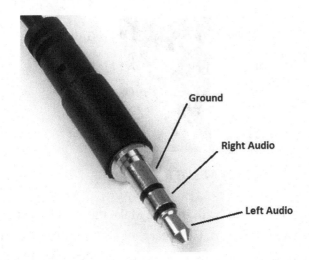

Ground

Right Audio

Left Audio

Figure 10-13. *Audio jack*

Voltage Regulator IC

Voltage regulator ICs automatically maintain a constant output voltage despite the input voltage changes. For instance, 7805 is a voltage regulator IC with 5 V output voltage. This IC can take an input voltage in the [7 V, 30 V] range and gives a constant 5 V output.

Most of digital circuits require a 5 V supply, and higher voltages destroy them. Therefore, you can use a 7805 voltage regulator IC (Figure 10-14) to supply these types of circuits.

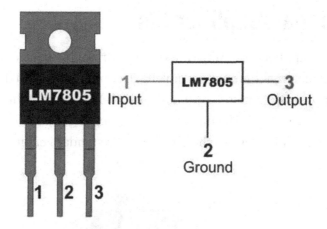

Figure 10-14. *Pinout of LM 7805*

The circuit shown in Figure 10-15 shows how to use 7805 IC. The unregulated input voltage enters the pin 1 and 5 V voltage is taken from pin 3.

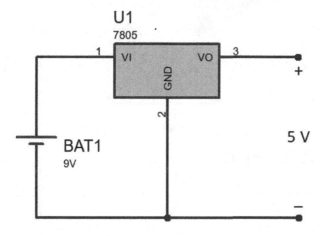

Figure 10-15. *5 V voltage regulator*

Operational Amplifier ICs

Operational amplifiers (Op Amp) are very important ICs in electronics. For instance, you can make amplifiers or voltage comparators with them. A very well-known Op Amp is shown in Figure 10-16. Pinout of this Op Amp is shown in Figure 10-17. The pin 8 is not connected (NC). There is nothing connected to this pin; it is just there to make it a standard eight-pin package.

Figure 10-16. *LM 741 IC*

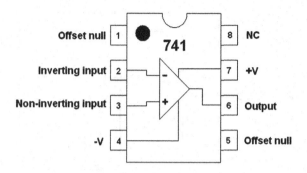

Figure 10-17. *Pinout of LM 741*

Let's make an amplifier with this IC. Make the circuit shown in Figure 10-18. Note that this circuit requires a symmetric power supply (i.e., requires both positive and negative voltages). Gain of this circuit is -10, and output voltage can be in the [-8.4 V, +8.4 V] range (the given range is approximate). For instance, if you apply 10 mV to the input terminal, you will have -100 mV at the output. If you apply -500 mV to the input, you will observe +5 V at the output. However, if you apply 1 V or 1.5 V as input, the output saturates, and it will stay at -8.4 V since it cannot be -10 V or -15 V.

Op Amp saturation occurs when the output voltage reaches its maximum or minimum limit and cannot increase or decrease any further. For instance, for the circuit shown in Figure 10-18, the input values outside the [-840 mV, +840 mV] cause saturation (Figure 10-19).

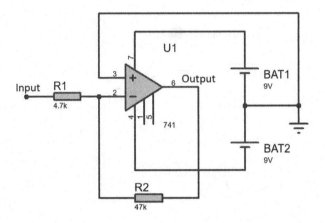

Figure 10-18. *An amplifier with gain of -10 ($\frac{V_{Output}}{V_{Input}} = -10$)*

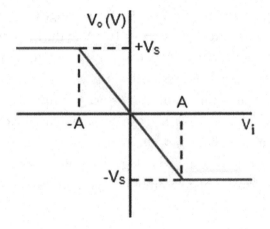

Figure 10-19. *Input-output relationship for circuit shown in Figure 10-18 (Vs≈8.4 V, A≈0.84 V)*

Let's test the circuit. Add the R3 and R4 to the circuit (Figure 10-20). Use a DC voltmeter to measure the input and output voltage (connect the black probe of the multimeter to the ground, and connect the red probe to the input and output nodes). Calculate the ratio of measured output voltage to measured input voltage. In Figure 10-20, the input voltage is small. Therefore, the Op Amp is in the linear region.

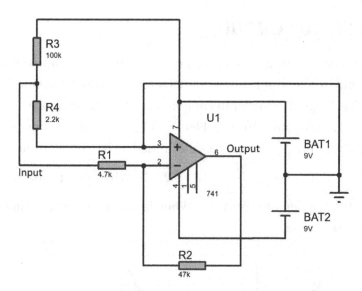

Figure 10-20. *Input of the circuit is supplied with a small DC voltage*

Let's repeat the experiment with R3 and R4 values shown in Figure 10-21. In Figure 10-21, the input voltage is big enough to saturate the Op Amp. Use a voltmeter to measure the output saturation voltage of the Op Amp.

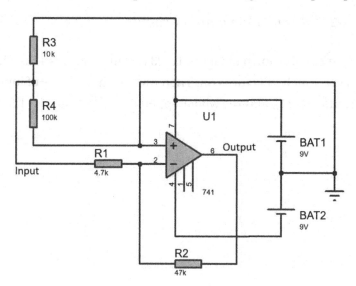

Figure 10-21. *R3=10 kΩ and R4=100 kΩ*

Comparator Circuit

An Op Amp can be used to make a comparator circuit. A comparator circuit compares an input voltage with a reference and determines whether it is bigger or smaller in comparison with the reference. For instance, the circuit shown in Figure 10-22 compares an input with 0.82 V reference (reference is determined by R1 and R2 values: $-9 + \dfrac{R2}{R1+R2} \times 18 = -9 + \dfrac{1.2k}{1k+1.2k} \times 18 = 0.82\ V$). When input voltage is bigger than 0.82 V, the green LED turns on. When input voltage is less than 0.82 V, the red LED turns on.

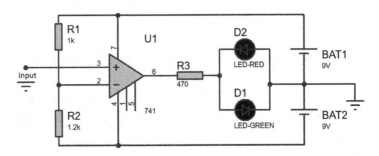

Figure 10-22. *A simple comparator circuit*

Make the circuit shown in Figure 10-23 (input voltage is +1.5 V in this case), and see which LED turns on. Then reverse the polarity of input voltage (Figure 10-24), and see what happens (input voltage is -1.5 V in this case).

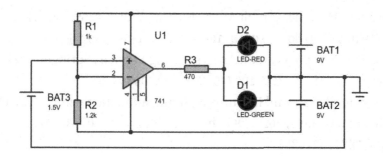

Figure 10-23. *+1.5 V is given to the + terminal of the Op Amp*

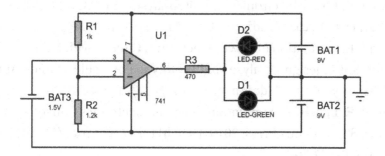

Figure 10-24. *-1.5 V is given to the + terminal of the Op Amp*

References for Further Study

[1] Asadi F., Analog Electronic Circuits Laboratory Manual, Springer, 2023. DOI: https://doi.org/10.1007/978-3-031-25122-1

[2] Asadi F., Digital Circuits Laboratory Manual, Springer, 2023. DOI: https://doi.org/10.1007/978-3-031-41516-6

[3] Asadi F., Electric Circuits Laboratory Manual, Springer, 2023. DOI: https://doi.org/10.1007/978-3-031-24552-7

[4] Asadi F., Eguchi K., Electronic Measurement: A Practical Approach, Springer, 2021. DOI: https://doi.org/10.1007/978-3-031-02021-6

[5] Asadi F., Essential Circuit Analysis using NI Multisim™ and MATLAB®, Springer, 2022. DOI: https://doi.org/10.1007/978-3-030-89850-2

[6]   Asadi F., Essential Circuit Analysis Using Proteus®, Springer, 2022. DOI: https://doi.org/10.1007/978-981-19-4353-9

[7]   Asadi F., Essential Circuit Analysis using LTspice®, Springer, 2022. DOI: https://doi.org/10.1007/978-3-031-09853-6

[8]   Asadi F., Electric and Electronic Circuit Simulation using TINA-TI®, River Publishers, 2022. DOI: https://doi.org/10.13052/rp-9788770226851

[9]   Asadi F., Electric Circuit Analysis with EasyEDA, Springer, 2022. DOI: https://doi.org/10.1007/978-3-031-00292-2

[10] Asadi F., Power Electronics Circuit Analysis with PSIM®, De Gruyter, 2021. DOI: https://doi.org/10.1515/9783110740653

[11] Asadi F., Simulation of Power Electronics Circuits with MATLAB®/Simulink®: Design, Analyze, and Prototype Power Electronics, Apress, 2022. DOI: https://doi.org/10.1007/978-1-4842-8220-5

[12] Asadi F., Eguchi K., Simulation of Power Electronics Converters Using PLECS®, Academic Press, 2019. DOI: https://doi.org/10.1016/C2018-0-02253-7

CHAPTER 11

Brushed Permanent Magnet DC Motors

A DC motor is an electric motor that uses direct current (DC) to produce mechanical force. DC motors have different types. This chapter focuses on the brushed permanent magnet DC motors. Permanent magnet DC motors have many applications. They are used in toys, automobile starters, wipers, shaving machines, hair dryers, robots, and many more.

Permanent magnet DC motors have two terminals. The motor starts rotating if you apply a DC voltage to its terminals. Speed of motor is directly proportional to the applied DC voltage: a bigger voltage leads to higher speed.

Several permanent magnet DC motors are shown in Figures 11-1, 11-2, and 11-3. Working principle of a DC motor is shown in [1].

Figure 11-1. *A typical DC motor*

© Farzin Asadi 2024
F. Asadi, *ABCs of Electronics*, Maker Innovations Series,
https://doi.org/10.1007/979-8-8688-0134-1_11

Figure 11-2. *A DC motor with gear box*

Figure 11-3. *Small DC motor with gear box*

Direction of Rotation

Permanent magnet DC motor starts to spin in one direction when you apply a DC voltage to its terminals (Figure 11-4).

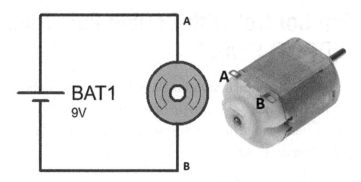

Figure 11-4. *DC motor spins when you apply a DC voltage to it*

When the polarity of applied voltage is reversed, the direction of the rotation is also reversed (Figure 11-5).

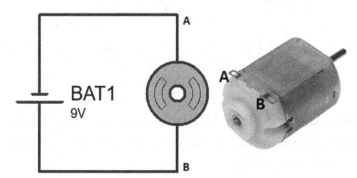

Figure 11-5. *The direction of rotation is opposite to that in Figure 11-4*

Thus, the polarity of applied voltage determines the motor direction, while the amplitude of voltage determines the speed of motor.

Direction Control with Double Pole Double Throw (DPDT) Switch

You can control the direction of rotation with double pole double throw (DPDT) switch. DPDT has two states: in one of the states, x is connected to a, and y is connected to c. In the other state, x is connected to b, and y is connected to d (Figure 11-6).

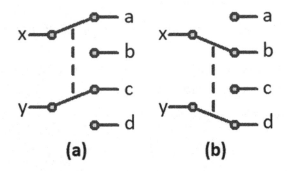

(a)   **(b)**

Figure 11-6. *Different states of a DPDT switch*

The circuit shown in Figure 11-7 can be used to control the direction of a motor. SW1 controls the motor direction, and SW2 turns the motor on/off. Explain how this circuit works.

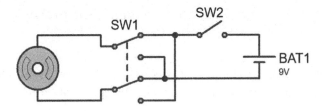

Figure 11-7. *Control of direction of rotation with DPDT switch*

Another solution for direction control is shown in Figure 11-8. Direction of rotation is controlled by the SW switch.

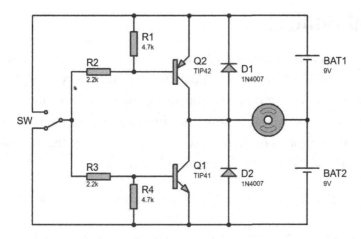

Figure 11-8. *An electronic circuit to control the direction of rotation of a small DC motor*

LED Direction Indicator

The circuit shown in Figure 11-9 can be used as a direction indicator for small permanent magnet DC motors. D1 turns on when the motor spins in one direction, and D2 turns on when the motor spins in the reverse direction. Explain how this circuit works.

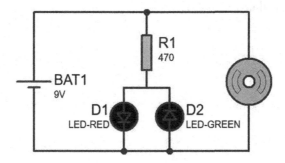

Figure 11-9. *A simple direction indicator for a small DC motor*

Speed Control

A simple solution for speed control of small DC motors is shown in Figure 11-10. When you press the push button, the battery voltage is directly applied to the motor, and the motor spins at its maximum speed. When you release the push button, the current passes through the diodes, and the voltage drop of each diode decreases the voltage that reaches the motor terminals. Therefore, the motor speed decreases.

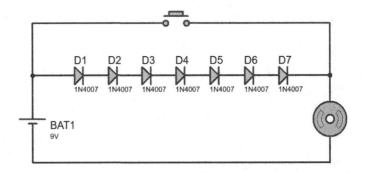

Figure 11-10. *A simple speed control circuit*

Circuit shown in Figure 11-11 is a more accurate solution for speed control problem of permanent magnet DC motors. Speed of the motor is controlled by the 50 kΩ potentiometer. This circuit uses a technique called pulse width modulation (PWM).

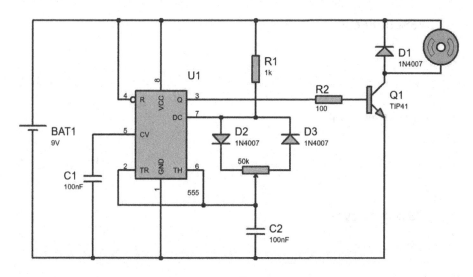

Figure 11-11. *PWM speed control circuit*

Let's see what PWM is. Consider the pulse shown in Figure 11-12.

Duty cycle (d) is defined as $d = \dfrac{T_{on}}{T_{on} + T_{off}} = \dfrac{T_{on}}{T}$. For instance, assume that

$T_{on} = 0.7$ *ms* and $T_{off} = 0.3$ *ms*. Therefore, $T_{on} + T_{off} = 1$ *ms*, and duty cycle is

$d = \dfrac{T_{on}}{T} = \dfrac{0.7\,ms}{1\,ms} = 0.7$ or 70%.

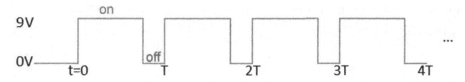

Figure 11-12. *A typical pulse*

Figure 11-13 shows several pulses with different duty cycles. Note that all of the pulses have the same frequency.

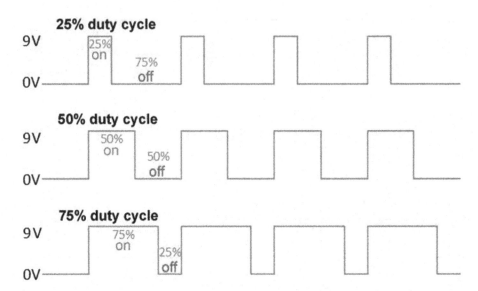

Figure 11-13. *Three pulses with 25%, 50%, and 75% duty cycles*

Assume that the pulses shown in Figure 11-13 are applied to a DC motor and speed of shaft is measured for each case. The pulse with 25% duty cycle generates the minimum speed, and the pulse with 75% duty cycle generates the maximum speed (when on duration increases the energy of the signal increases).

The circuit shown in Figure 11-11 adjusts the duty cycle of the pulses applied to the motor. Duty cycle of pulses is controlled by the 50 kΩ potentiometer.

References for Further Study

[1]   https://www.youtube.com/watch?v=CWulQ1ZSE3c

[2]   Asadi F., Analog Electronic Circuits Laboratory Manual, Springer, 2023. DOI: https://doi.org/10.1007/978-3-031-25122-1

[3] Asadi F., Digital Circuits Laboratory Manual, Springer, 2023.
DOI: https://doi.org/10.1007/978-3-031-41516-6

[4] Asadi F., Electric Circuits Laboratory Manual, Springer, 2023.
DOI: https://doi.org/10.1007/978-3-031-24552-7

[5] Asadi F., Eguchi K., Electronic Measurement: A Practical Approach,
Springer, 2021. DOI: https://doi.org/10.1007/978-3-031-02021-6

[6] Asadi F., Essential Circuit Analysis using NI Multisim™ and MATLAB®,
Springer, 2022. DOI: https://doi.org/10.1007/978-3-030-89850-2

[7] Asadi F., Essential Circuit Analysis Using Proteus®, Springer, 2022.
DOI: https://doi.org/10.1007/978-981-19-4353-9

[8] Asadi F., Essential Circuit Analysis using LTspice®, Springer, 2022.
DOI: https://doi.org/10.1007/978-3-031-09853-6

[9] Asadi F., Electric and Electronic Circuit Simulation using TINA-TI®,
River Publishers, 2022. DOI: https://doi.org/10.13052/
rp-9788770226851

[10] Asadi F., Electric Circuit Analysis with EasyEDA, Springer, 2022.
DOI: https://doi.org/10.1007/978-3-031-00292-2

[11] Asadi F., Power Electronics Circuit Analysis with PSIM®, De Gruyter,
2021. DOI: https://doi.org/10.1515/9783110740653

[12] Asadi F., Simulation of Power Electronics Circuits with MATLAB®/
Simulink®: Design, Analyze, and Prototype Power Electronics, Apress,
2022. DOI: https://doi.org/10.1007/978-1-4842-8220-5

[13] Asadi F., Eguchi K., Simulation of Power Electronics Converters Using
PLECS®, Academic Press, 2019. DOI: https://doi.org/10.1016/
C2018-0-02253-7

CHAPTER 12

Digital Electronics

A signal for conveying information which is a continuous function of time is known as analog signal (Figure 12-1). A digital signal is a signal that represents data as a sequence of binary values (Figure 12-2). In each instant of time, a digital signal can take only one of the two values. The allowed two values are called high and low or 1 and 0. A digital system is a system that works with digital signals.

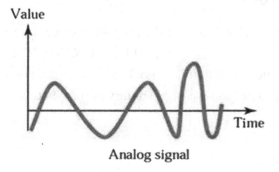

Figure 12-1. *An analog signal*

© Farzin Asadi 2024

F. Asadi, *ABCs of Electronics*, Maker Innovations Series,
https://doi.org/10.1007/979-8-8688-0134-1_12

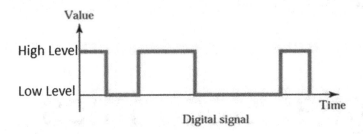

Figure 12-2. *A digital signal*

This chapter introduces the basic concepts of digital systems gently. Refer to the references given at the end of the chapter if you want to learn more about the subject.

Logic Gates

Logic gates are building blocks of digital systems. Logic gates perform basic logic functions like AND, OR, XOR, NOT, NAND, NOR, and XNOR. A logic gate is a device that performs a logical operation on one or more binary inputs and produces a single binary output. Let's study the logic gates with more details.

AND Gate

Symbol of AND gate is shown in Figure 12-3. It has two inputs and one output.

Figure 12-3. *Symbol of AND gate*

Input-output relationship for this gate is shown in Table 12-1.

Table 12-1. *Input-output relationship for AND gate*

Input A	Input B	Output Q
Low	Low	Low
Low	High	Low
High	Low	Low
High	High	High

AND gates behave like a series circuit (Figure 12-4).

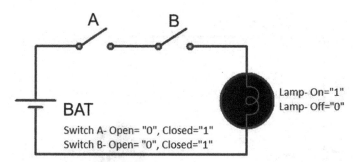

Figure 12-4. *The behavior of a series circuit is similar to an AND gate*

OR Gate

Symbol of OR gate is shown in Figure 12-5. It has two inputs and one output.

Figure 12-5. *Symbol of OR gate*

Input-output relationship for this gate is shown in Table 12-2.

Table 12-2. *Input-output relationship for OR gate*

Input A	Input B	Output Q
Low	Low	Low
Low	High	High
High	Low	High
High	High	High

OR gates behave like a parallel circuit (Figure 12-6).

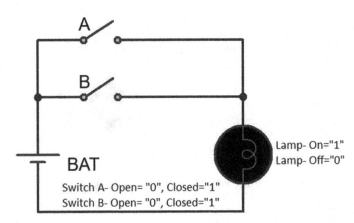

Figure 12-6. *The behavior of a parallel circuit is similar to an OR gate*

XOR (Exclusive OR) Gate

Symbol of XOR gate is shown in Figure 12-7. It has two inputs and one output.

Figure 12-7. *Symbol of XOR gate*

Input-output relationship for this gate is shown in Table 12-3.

Table 12-3. *Input-output relationship for XOR gate*

Input A	Input B	Output Q
Low	Low	Low
Low	High	High
High	Low	High
High	High	Low

NOT Gate

Symbol of NOT gate is shown in Figure 12-8. It has one input and one output. The NOT gate inverts (complements) its input signal.

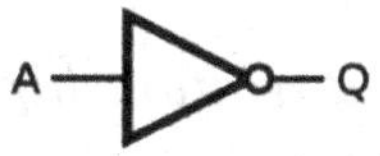

Figure 12-8. *Symbol of NOT gate*

Input-output relationship for this gate is shown in Table 12-4.

Table 12-4. *Input-output relationship for NOT gate*

Input A	Output Q
Low	High
High	Low

NAND Gate

Symbol of NAND gate is shown in Figure 12-9. It has two inputs and one output.

Figure 12-9. *Symbol of NAND gate*

Figure 12-10 shows the equivalent circuit for NAND gate. The NAND gate is the complement of the AND gate.

Figure 12-10. *Equivalent circuit for NAND gate*

Input-output relationship for this gate is shown in Table 12-5.

Table 12-5. *Input-output relationship for NAND gate. Compare it with Table 12-1*

Input A	Input B	Output Q
Low	Low	High
Low	High	Low
High	Low	Low
High	High	Low

NOR Gate

Symbol of NOR gate is shown in Figure 12-11. It has two inputs and one output.

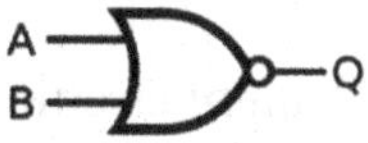

Figure 12-11. *Symbol of NOR gate*

Figure 12-12 shows the equivalent circuit for NOR gate. The NOR gate is the complement of the OR gate.

Figure 12-12. *Equivalent circuit for NOR gate*

Input-output relationship for this gate is shown in Table 12-6. Compare it with Table 12-2.

Table 12-6. *Input-output relationship for NOR gate*

Input A	Input B	Output Q
Low	Low	High
Low	High	Low
High	Low	Low
High	High	Low

XNOR Gate

Symbol of XNOR gate is shown in Figure 12-13. It has two inputs and one output.

Figure 12-13. *Symbol of XNOR gate*

Figure 12-14 shows the equivalent circuit for XNOR gate. The XNOR gate is the complement of the XOR gate.

Figure 12-14. *Equivalent circuit for XNOR gate*

Input-output relationship for this gate is shown in Table 12-7. Compare it with Table 12-3.

Table 12-7. *Input-output relationship for XNOR gate*

Input A	Input B	Output Q
Low	Low	High
Low	High	Low
High	Low	Low
High	High	High

TTL (Transistor Transistor Logic) ICs

Small and medium scale (SSI and MSI) logic IC families are currently made in a wide range of subfamilies and a variety of package types, using three different technologies:

A) TTL (transistor transistor logic)

B) CMOS (complementary metal-oxide semiconductor)

C) ECL (emitter coupled logic)

Only TTL ICs are studied here. More information about CMOS and ECL can be found in [1]. TTL ICs start with 74 and can work in 0°C up to 70°C. TTL ICs have the GND and VCC pins in the left bottom and right top pins (Figure 12-15). VCC and GND are power supply connections of the IC. VCC and GND are connected to + and - terminals of the power supply, respectively. TTL ICs are feed with 5 V. Voltages bigger than +5 V destroy the IC. High and low levels for TTL ICs are +5 V and 0 V, respectively.

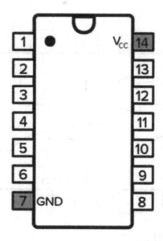

Figure 12-15. *Common position of VCC and ground pins*

Pinouts of some of commonly used digital ICs are shown in Figures 12-16, 12-17, 12-18, 12-19, and 12-20.

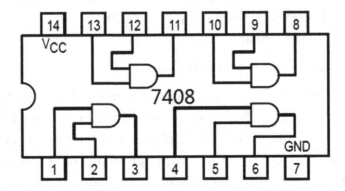

Figure 12-16. *Pinout of 7408*

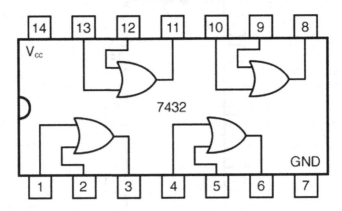

Figure 12-17. *Pinout of 7432*

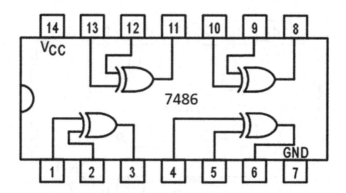

Figure 12-18. *Pinout of 7486*

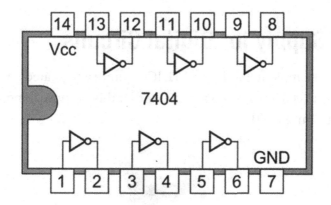

Figure 12-19. *Pinout of 7404*

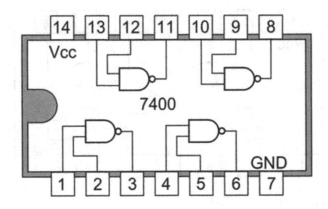

Figure 12-20. *Pinout of 7400*

Power Supply for Digital Circuits

Digital circuits implemented with TTL ICs require a regulated 5 V supply. You can use a 7805 linear voltage regulator for this purpose. Pinout of 7805 is shown in Figure 12-21.

1: Input
2: GND
3: Output

Figure 12-21. *Pinout of 7805 voltage regulator IC*

The circuit shown in Figure 12-22 shows how to make a 5 V regulated power supply with 7805 IC.

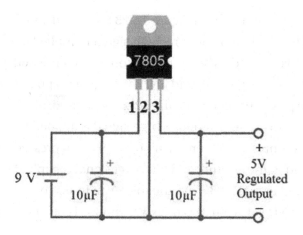

Figure 12-22. *A simple 5 V power supply*

Sample Circuit with Digital ICs

Let's see how logic gates work. Make the circuit shown in Figure 12-23 on a breadboard. Leave the pin 4, 5, 6, 8, 9, 10, 11, 12, and 13 open. These pins are not used in this experiment. This experiment shows how AND gate works.

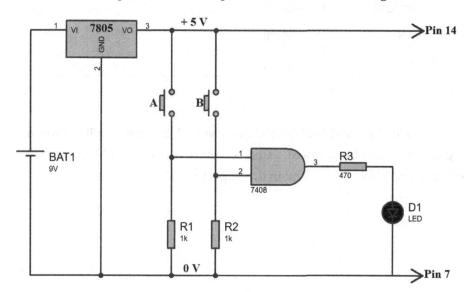

Figure 12-23. *Test circuit for AND gate*

179

When the push button A in Figure 12-23 is pressed, pin 1 of 7408 IC is connected to +5 V line. Therefore, high signal is applied to pin 1 when push button A is pressed. When push button A is not pressed, pin 1 of the IC is connected to the ground, and low level signal is applied to pin 1.

When the push button B in Figure 12-23 is pressed, pin 2 of 7408 IC is connected to +5 V line. Therefore, high signal is applied to pin 2 when push button A is pressed. When push button B is not pressed, pin 2 of the IC is connected to the ground, and low level signal is applied to pin 2.

The LED in Figure 12-23 plays the role of an indicator. When LED is on, the output of AND gate (pin 3) is high. When LED is off, the output of AND gate is low.

Complete Table 12-8 and compare it with Table 12-1.

Table 12-8. *Input-output relationship for circuit shown in Figure 12-23*

Push button A	Push button B	Output (LED)
Not pressed	Not pressed	
Not pressed	Pressed	
Pressed	Not pressed	
Pressed	Pressed	

Let's continue and see how OR gates work. Make the circuit shown in Figure 12-24 on a breadboard. Leave the pin 4, 5, 6, 8, 9, 10, 11, 12, and 13 open. These pins are not used in this experiment.

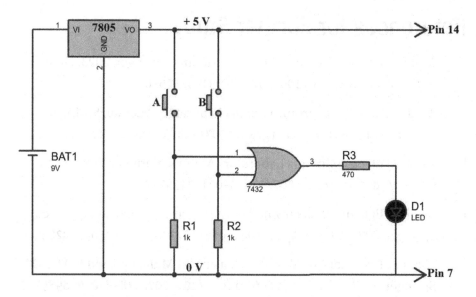

Figure 12-24. *Test circuit for OR gate*

Fill Table 12-9 and compare it with Table 12-2.

Table 12-9. *Input-output relationship for circuit shown in Figure 12-24*

Push button A	Push button B	Output (LED)
Not pressed	Not pressed	
Not pressed	Pressed	
Pressed	Not pressed	
Pressed	Pressed	

Continue this experiment, and obtain the input-output relationship for 7486, 7404, and 7400 ICs as well.

References for Further Study

[1]   Asadi F., Digital Circuits Laboratory Manual, Springer, 2023. DOI:
      https://doi.org/10.1007/978-3-031-41516-6

[2]   Asadi F., Analog Electronic Circuits Laboratory Manual, Springer,
      2023. DOI: https://doi.org/10.1007/978-3-031-25122-1

[3]   Asadi F., Electric Circuits Laboratory Manual, Springer, 2023. DOI:
      https://doi.org/10.1007/978-3-031-24552-7

[4]   Asadi F., Eguchi K., Electronic Measurement: A Practical Approach,
      Springer, 2021. DOI: https://doi.org/10.1007/978-3-031-02021-6

[5]   Asadi F., Essential Circuit Analysis using NI Multisim™ and MATLAB®,
      Springer, 2022. DOI: https://doi.org/10.1007/978-3-030-89850-2

[6]   Asadi F., Essential Circuit Analysis Using Proteus®, Springer, 2022.
      DOI: https://doi.org/10.1007/978-981-19-4353-9

[7]   Asadi F., Essential Circuit Analysis using LTspice®, Springer, 2022. DOI:
      https://doi.org/10.1007/978-3-031-09853-6

[8]   Asadi F., Electric and Electronic Circuit Simulation using TINA-TI®,
      River Publishers, 2022. DOI: https://doi.org/10.13052/
      rp-9788770226851

[9]   Asadi F., Electric Circuit Analysis with EasyEDA, Springer, 2022. DOI:
      https://doi.org/10.1007/978-3-031-00292-2

[10] Asadi F., Power Electronics Circuit Analysis with PSIM®, De Gruyter,
      2021. DOI: https://doi.org/10.1515/9783110740653

[11] Asadi F., Simulation of Power Electronics Circuits with MATLAB®/
Simulink®: Design, Analyze, and Prototype Power Electronics, Apress,
2022. DOI: https://doi.org/10.1007/978-1-4842-8220-5

[12] Asadi F., Eguchi K., Simulation of Power Electronics Converters Using
PLECS®, Academic Press, 2019. DOI: https://doi.org/10.1016/
C2018-0-02253-7

CHAPTER 13

Measurement Devices

Digital multimeter and oscilloscopes are two important measurement devices that are used in electronics engineering. This chapter introduces these two measurement devices. There exist many other measurement devices; however, this chapter introduces only digital multimeter and oscilloscope. Refer to the end of chapter references to obtain more information about measurement devices.

Multimeters

Multimeters are one of the most commonly used measurement devices. They can measure resistance, voltage (AC or DC), current (AC or DC), and in some models temperature, frequency, voltage drop of diodes, and capacitance. Multimeters could be divided into two categories: analog multimeters and digital multimeters (DMMs).

Analog multimeters have a moving pointer and a scale in order to show the measurement result (Figure 13-1). Digital multimeters don't have any moving parts, but rather a display in order to show the result. Analog multimeters are obsolete today, and because of that, we only study the DMMs.

© Farzin Asadi 2024
F. Asadi, *ABCs of Electronics*, Maker Innovations Series,
https://doi.org/10.1007/979-8-8688-0134-1_13

Figure 13-1. *An analog multimeter*

Different types of DMMs are made. Some types are designed to be portable (Figure 13-2). These types are supplied from a battery and are lightweight. Another commonly used type is the desktop DMM (Figure 13-3) which is designed to be supplied from city electricity.

Figure 13-2. *Portable DMM*

Figure 13-3. *Desktop DMM*

The price of DMMs depends on the accuracy of the device and varies from a few dollars up to thousands of dollars. Needless to say, the more accurate devices are more expensive. DMMs could be divided into two groups: "switched" multimeters and "auto-range" multimeters.

In switched multimeters, selection of the suitable range for measurement is the duty of user; however, in auto-range multimeters, this job is done automatically by the device itself. Figures 13-4 and 13-5 show the switched and auto-range multimeters, respectively.

Figure 13-4. *A switched DMM*

Figure 13-5. *An auto-range DMM*

Assume that you want to measure the voltage of a car battery with the DMM shown in Figure 13-4. You need to put the selector in the DC voltage measurement section and select a suitable range based on the value which you want to measure. We know that a nominal value of a car battery is 12 V DC. So, the 20 V range is a good option for this measurement because the measured value is less than 20 V. Note that you can use 200 V or 500 V ranges for this measurement as well. However, your measurement will not be precise. The maximum precision is given by the 20 V range. For instance, when the 20 V range is selected, you read 11.3 V. However, when you use the 200 V or 500 V range, you may see 11 or 12 V on the display.

Always start with the maximum available measurement range if you do not have any idea about the magnitude of voltage/current under measurement. This gives you a good approximation without destroying the measurement device. Now you can select a better measurement range to obtain the best precision.

Oscilloscopes

The oscilloscope is the most important measurement device in electronics engineering. Oscilloscopes permit you to see the voltage waveforms.

Oscilloscopes can be classified into two groups: analog oscilloscopes and digital oscilloscopes. An analog oscilloscope and a digital oscilloscope are shown in Figures 13-6 and 13-7, respectively.

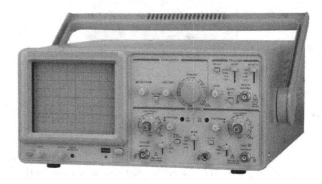

Figure 13-6. *An analog oscilloscope*

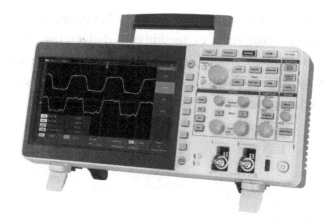

Figure 13-7. *A digital oscilloscope*

Analog oscilloscopes use a cathode ray tube (CRT) in order to show the waveforms. A CRT sample is shown in Figure 13-8.

Figure 13-8. *CRT of an analog oscilloscope*

A CRT is a glass envelope which is deep, heavy, and fragile. The interior is evacuated to approximately 0.01 pascal to 133 nanopascal to facilitate the free flight of electrons from the gun(s) to the tube's face without scattering due to collisions with air molecules. The face is typically made of thick lead glass or special barium-strontium glass to be shatter-resistant and to block most X-ray emissions. CRTs make up most of the weight of an analog oscilloscope.

The structure of CRT is shown in Figure 13-9. The input waveform to the oscilloscope with the aid of deflecting coils deflects the electron beam coming from the heated cathode, and after the electrons hit the fluorescent screen, an image appears on the screen. Analog oscilloscopes are heavier than digital oscilloscopes.

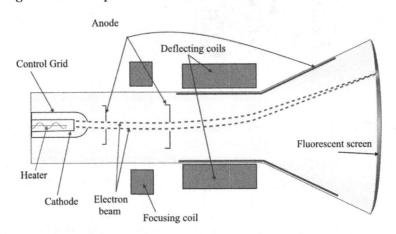

Figure 13-9. *Structure of CRT*

Digital oscilloscopes do not use CRT. In digital oscilloscopes, signals are shown on a liquid crystal display (LCD). Digital oscilloscopes use an analog to digital converter (ADC) in order to sample the input waveform (Figure 13-10). Generated samples are used to form the image on the screen.

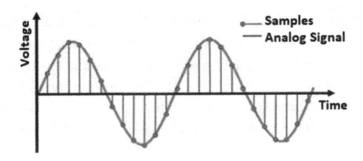

Figure 13-10. *Sampling an analog signal*

Digital oscilloscopes are more flexible than analog ones. They can do a lot of measurements automatically. For instance, they can measure RMS or average value of a complex signal, duty ratio of pulses, peak-to-peak voltage, settling time of waveforms, etc. These days, the price of a digital oscilloscope is quite affordable. So, they have taken the place of analog oscilloscopes.

References for Further Study

[1]   Asadi F., Analog Electronic Circuits Laboratory Manual, Springer, 2023. DOI: https://doi.org/10.1007/978-3-031-25122-1

[2]   Asadi F., Digital Circuits Laboratory Manual, Springer, 2023. DOI: https://doi.org/10.1007/978-3-031-41516-6

[3]   Asadi F., Electric Circuits Laboratory Manual, Springer, 2023. DOI: https://doi.org/10.1007/978-3-031-24552-7

[4]   Asadi F., Eguchi K., Electronic Measurement: A Practical Approach, Springer, 2021. DOI: https://doi.org/10.1007/978-3-031-02021-6

[5]   Asadi F., Essential Circuit Analysis using NI Multisim™ and MATLAB®, Springer, 2022. DOI: https://doi.org/10.1007/978-3-030-89850-2

[6]   Asadi F., Essential Circuit Analysis Using Proteus®, Springer, 2022. DOI: https://doi.org/10.1007/978-981-19-4353-9

[7]   Asadi F., Essential Circuit Analysis using LTspice®, Springer, 2022. DOI: https://doi.org/10.1007/978-3-031-09853-6

[8]   Asadi F., Electric and Electronic Circuit Simulation using TINA-TI®, River Publishers, 2022. DOI: https://doi.org/10.13052/rp-9788770226851

[9]   Asadi F., Electric Circuit Analysis with EasyEDA, Springer, 2022. DOI: https://doi.org/10.1007/978-3-031-00292-2

[10] Asadi F., Power Electronics Circuit Analysis with PSIM®, De Gruyter, 2021. DOI: https://doi.org/10.1515/9783110740653

[11] Asadi F., Simulation of Power Electronics Circuits with MATLAB®/
      Simulink®: Design, Analyze, and Prototype Power Electronics, Apress,
      2022. DOI: https://doi.org/10.1007/978-1-4842-8220-5

[12] Asadi F., Eguchi K., Simulation of Power Electronics Converters Using
      PLECS®, Academic Press, 2019. DOI: https://doi.org/10.1016/
      C2018-0-02253-7

Index

© Farzin Asadi 2024
F. Asadi, *ABCs of Electronics*, Maker Innovations Series,
https://doi.org/10.1007/979-8-8688-0134-1

base, collector, and emitter
terminals, 103, 104
directions of current flow,
104, 105
internal structure, 100, 102
symbol, 102, 103

O

Ohm's law, 44, 51, 53
Op Amp saturation, 151
Operational amplifiers (Op
Amp), 150–153
OR gate, 169, 170
Oscilloscopes, 190

P

P-channel MOSFETs, 125, 126
Permanent magnet DC motors
applications, 157
direction of rotation,
158, 159
gear box, 158
LED direction indicator, 161
speed control, 162–164
terminals, 157
working principle, 157
Pinout, 106, 127, 138, 139, 144, 146,
147, 150, 151, 175–178
Positive temperature coefficient
(NTC) thermistors, 66
Potentiometer
audio/video devices, 61

definition, 60
resistive element, 60
structure, 60
symbol, 61
variable resistor, 61, 62
wiper, 60
Power supply (PS)
adaptors, 4
mains electricity, 1
Pulse width modulation
(PWM), 162
Push button, 40
Push button switch, 25
calculators, 26
car horn, 27
door bell, 25
remote controls, 26
symbol, 27
PWM speed control circuit, 163

Q

Quad-flat no-leads (QFN), 95, 142
Quad-flat package (QFP), 95, 142

R

Relays
DPDT, 136
DPST, 136
electromagnet, 133–135
electromechanical switch, 133
ferromagnetic or ferromagnetic
material, 134

Printed in the United States
by Baker & Taylor Publisher Services